The Book of Great
Breakfasts and Brunches

The Book of Great Breakfasts and Brunches

Terence Janericco

CBI Publishing Company, Inc.
286 Congress Street
Boston, Massachusetts 02210

Production Editor / Becky Handler
Text Designer / Designed For:
Compositor / Arrow Composition
Jacket Designer / Christy Rosso
Cover Photography / John Carrier

Library of Congress Cataloging in Publication Data

Janericco, Terence.
  The book of great breakfasts and brunches.

  Includes index.
  1. Breakfasts. 2. Brunches. I. Title.
TX733.J357 1983   641.5′2   82-24461
ISBN 0-8436-2264-4

This book is dedicated to the members of my family who have borne with me over these many years as I have learned to cook.

For my parents, Helen and Jacob Janericco.

For my brothers, Thomas and Theodore.

Contents

Chapter 10

Chapter 11

Chapter 12

Appendix

Preface

Brunches, a distinctly American form of entertaining, have become increasingly popular in the last twenty years. At brunch, a group of friends can gather for a casual, inexpensive meal.

Brunches fall into two categories, but the differences are not always clear. Some brunches are truly breakfasts, held early in the day, with the emphasis solely on breakfast foods. Others are actually lunches, even though they may be the first meal of the day for some, and the food is more substantial with greater variety. Consider first which meal you want to emphasize: whether you want to rely more on lunch or on breakfast. In addition, it may be necessary to consider the waking hours of your guests.

Whatever the emphasis, select a menu that allows much of the work to be done ahead. Getting up at 5:00 A.M. to make croissants is no fun. When arranging a brunch, no matter how casual, organization is the key to a relaxed meal. Remember that brunch is supposed to be an easy meal, not only for your guests but also for you! With careful planning, you can serve delicious meals with a minimum of effort. Most of the recipes in this book instruct you how to prepare the food ahead and how to keep it until ready to serve. Some foods simply must be made and served. For example, omelets cannot be prepared ahead or frozen. But, if the other tasks are done ahead, you will be free to prepare the omelets to order.

In addition to preparing much of the food ahead, you can set the table, arrange the flowers, and set up the bar, except for the ice, the night before. Any lemons and limes needed for the drinks can also be cut and stored, covered, in the refrigerator.

Brunches can be extremely informal, with everyone in the kitchen helping to put things together and making their own omelets or pancakes; they can also be very formal affairs with uniformed servers passing cheese pastries before the guests sit down to creamed lobster. Most brunches fall somewhere in between.

Since brunches are supposed to be light, interesting meals that satisfy people's appetites pleasantly, do not offer too many food choices at one meal or too many rich and filling dishes, just to display your skills. Remember, if you are relaxed, your guests will be too.

CHAPTER 1
Beverages

Depending on the hour, a brunch may or may not start with quantities of freshly ground, freshly brewed, piping hot coffee. Instant coffee is never acceptable, especially for a party, no matter how informal. True coffee lovers will appreciate carefully selected, freshly ground beans. If you do not have a grinder, have the coffee ground at the store. There are many coffees from which to choose and you can taste test the varieties to select your preference. In time, you can learn to mix different coffees to achieve your personal blend.

Tea lovers often do not drink coffee but they deserve as much consideration as coffee drinkers. Do them the honor of brewing an honest pot of tea. It really is quite simple. You can also blend teas to suit your taste, or serve any of the numerous flavored teas. Do consider your guests; just because someone drinks tea does not mean that they drink any herb or root steeped in hot water!

On winter weekends, in particular, but at other times as well, hot cocoa is delightful for breakfast or brunch. It can be made ahead and reheated gently before serving it, something you cannot do with coffee or tea. Cocoa can be as sweet and milky or dark and bitter as you wish.

A well-chilled, perfectly made Bloody Mary is, for many people, the only acceptable brunch drink. Bloody Marys are delicious and should be available. However, there are numerous other drinks to serve. Orange juice can be combined with almost any alcohol to start the day as a Screw Driver, Golden Gate, Orange Blossom, or Bucks Fizz.

Generally, alcoholic drinks for brunch are based on fruit or vegetable juices. They should be moderately low in alcoholic content. If the meal is more of a lunch than a breakfast, wine may be in order. Champagne, of course, is the perfect breakfast-brunch drink, but serve extra dry rather than brut (it mixes well with fruit and slightly sweet breads). This is not the hour to serve the most expensive wines. Enjoy some of the less familiar vineyards and varieties that do not fit perfectly into other meals, particularly the less expensive wines of the Rhine and Mosel, which are light, crisp, and slightly fruity.

COFFEE

There are many ways of making coffee, and new machines appear on the market every year that are designed to help you make better coffee. Choose a method and a machine that pleases you. Generally, if there is a problem, it is not with the machine or method, but rather with the type of bean used and the grind. The author prefers to use a simple plastic cone with a paper filter set over a coffee pot. Water brought to a full rolling boil is poured slowly over finely ground coffee in the filter.

Coffee comes in many varieties from all over the world. Some beans are richer and more full flavored than others; some are lightly roasted, others are roasted longer to obtain deeper, richer flavors. My favorite combination is one quarter espresso, one quarter French roast, and one half Columbian Supremo. Mix the beans in a container and grind them as needed. This process produces a rich, full-flavored coffee with body. Other coffee drinkers may find this blend too full flavored.

One pound of coffee should yield 50 cups. Restaurants, when coffee prices are up, have tried unsuccessfully to stretch the coffee by making 60 and even 70 cups from a pound. Individuals should plan to make adjustments in quantities based on the type of coffee used and the strength preferred.

Coffee deserves some care, especially after the beans have been ground. They start to lose potency quickly. Ideally, keep whole bean coffee in the freezer. Remove the beans you will use in a week's time (purists insist that they be kept in the refrigerator) and grind enough for each pot. If you bought the coffee ground, definitely store it in the freezer if it is to be kept for any length of time. If it is tightly sealed and used in two or three days, freezing is unnecessary. Interestingly, one school of thought believes that coffee should be ground the night before and left exposed to the air to obtain its peak of perfection.

Coffee

---

2 quarts cold water   ⅔ cup coffee beans

Place the water in a kettle and bring to a full boil. Finely grind the beans and place in a paper filter and cone over a coffee pot. Pour on ½ cup of boiling water to moisten the grounds. When it has filtered through, add another ½ cup. Continue, ½ cup at a time, letting it seep through before adding more. Serve at once.

Yields 8 cups.

Note: This is the author's method. You should experiment to determine the method that works best for you.

Coffee is at its best made, served, and drunk within a half hour. This may not be practical for large groups. Once the coffee has been made, remove the grounds. If you must reheat it, do so gently. It should never come close to a boil once it has been made.

Serve coffee with cream and sugar. Heavy cream makes the richest coffee, but many people have acquired a taste for medium or light cream, and even milk. If you wish, offer sweetened whipped cream, possibly flavored with cinnamon, nutmeg, vanilla, or cloves. When serving a large crowd, mix 1 quart of milk with 1 cup of heavy cream for every 50 servings. You can make a richer mixture by increasing the amount of cream.

"Doctoring" coffee with spirits can be fun at a brunch. Set out an array of decanters with cognac, rum, whiskey, or orange liqueur, and allow guests to mix their own. Or serve Irish coffee or one of the other "spirited" coffees.

TEA

There are many blends and types of tea. Orange pekoe is the standard variety found in supermarkets and in most tea bags. True tea lovers detest tea bags, as much for their appearance as their flavor. Firms that sell premium coffees usually sell premium teas in many varieties and some interesting combinations of tea leaves and other flavorings, such as orange and ginger. It is also possible to purchase many varieties of herbal teas and *tisanes*. Serve exotic teas only when you know your guests enjoy them. If you are not knowledgeable about teas, consult with your dealer. Also, remember that your favorite herb tea may not be as well liked by your guests.

Tea should be kept in an airtight canister and used within a reasonable length of time. If you do not drink tea and have had it on the shelf longer than you can remember, discard it. Generally, teas keep about a year. If they are flavored (with oranges, etc.), they can lose their potency more quickly.

Tea

---

8 cups cold, fresh water   8 teaspoons loose tea

In a kettle, bring the water to a boil.

Pour two cups of water into the pot, swirl to heat the pot, and drain. Add the tea to the pot and pour on the remaining boiling water. Cover and steep for 3 to 5 minutes. Strain and serve with sugar and lemon or milk.

Yields 8 cups.

Like coffee, it is possible to lace tea with liquor. Have a decanter of rum or brandy available for guests to add to their tea, if they desire. Honey can be served to sweeten the tea.

COCOA

Although cocoa is not very popular as a breakfast drink in the United States, it is in Europe, especially in France and Spain. If you are giving a breakfast on a cold blustery day, cocoa can be a warm and soothing change.

Cocoa should be made from pure cocoa and not a mix. A mix can be prepared more quickly but allows you no control. Some people like their chocolate dark and bitter with an edge to it, and others want it milky and very sweet. By using pure cocoa, you can make it to suit any taste.

Cocoa

---

3 tablespoons cocoa
¼ cup sugar
pinch of salt

¾ cup of boiling water
4 cups milk

In a 2-quart saucepan, combine the cocoa, sugar, and salt. Stir in the water and cook, stirring, over medium heat for 2 minutes. Stir in the milk. With a rotary beater, wire whisk, or hand-held electric mixer, beat the mixture until foamy. This beating, called *milling,* prevents scum from forming on the surface.

Yields 8 cups.

Serve cocoa with a bowl of whipped cream, sweetened and flavored with vanilla, cinnamon, or cloves to your taste. You can also flavor the cream with rum or cognac. If you wish to change the proportion of cocoa and sugar for more or less flavor, do so. If you want a richer mixture, you can substitute cream for all or part of the milk. However, you must first cook the cocoa with the water to cook the starch before adding the milk or cream.

Cocoa can be cooled, refrigerated, and kept overnight to be reheated gently the following morning. Any scum that forms should be removed and discarded. The milling process should be done just before serving. Cocoa, like tea and coffee, can also benefit from a lacing of liqueur. Cognac and rum are two of the most popular, but orange liqueur or kirsch is a delectable change.

ALCOHOLIC BEVERAGES

Although the following recipes specify a particular liquor, they can often be made successfully with another liquor. Traditionally, a Bloody Mary is made with vodka, but it can also be made with gin or rum. Be adventuresome, but taste test your creation before offering it to your guests.

Glasses

The glass in which a particular drink is served is often a tradition. The most popular are the highball, old-fashioned, and wine glasses. Today, people feel less obligated to use a particular shape with a particular drink. These recipes indicate the size of the glass, but not the shape. The author usually serves drinks in oversized (18-ounce) wine glasses, whether they are straight up, on-the-rocks, with soda, or simply wine. There is room in such a glass for a lot of ice and room for the drink to be swirled.

Before you serve anything to your guests, a head straightener, stomach settler, or pick-me-up may be in order. The following recipe has been in the literature for close to a century. The author does not attest to its efficacy.

Prairie Oyster

1 egg yolk	¼ teaspoon vinegar
1 teaspoon catsup	black pepper to taste
1 teaspoon Worcestershire sauce	dash of cayenne, optional

Slide the egg yolk into an old-fashioned glass without breaking the yolk. Add the catsup, Worcestershire, and vinegar. Sprinkle with pepper. Drink in one gulp without breaking the yolk.

Yields 1 drink.

Although gin was the basis for most cocktails in past years, vodka seems to have taken precedence, and statistics indicate a definite increase in the use of rum, specifically light or white rum.

Fizzes are a wonderful brunch drink, light and refreshing, with a number of variations. Although these fizz recipes are written for gin, they can be made with rum or vodka.

Albemarle Fizz

1 tablespoon lemon juice	6 ounces soda water
½ tablespoon confectioners' sugar	1 teaspoon raspberry syrup
1 ounce gin	

In a blender, combine the lemon juice, sugar, and gin. Blend well. Pour into an 8-ounce glass. Fill with ice cubes and add the soda and raspberry syrup.

Yields 1 drink.

Gin Fizz

3 ounces gin	1 teaspoon confectioners' sugar
1½ ounces lemon juice	2 ounces soda water

In a blender, combine the gin, lemon juice, and sugar. Blend well. Pour into a 10-ounce, ice-filled glass and add the soda.

Yields 1 drink.

Golden Fizz

Add 1 whole egg to the blender in the Gin Fizz recipe and finish as directed.

Yields 1 drink.

Orange Fizz

3 ounces gin	1 teaspoon confectioners' sugar
3 ounces orange juice	2 ounces soda water
1½ ounces lemon or lime juice	

In a blender, combine the gin, orange juice, lemon or lime juice, and sugar. Blend well. Pour into an ice-filled glass and add the soda.

Yields 1 drink.

Bronx Cocktail

1 ounce gin	½ ounce sweet vermouth
1 ounce orange juice	½ ounce dry vermouth

In a blender, combine the gin, orange juice, and vermouths. Blend 20 seconds. Pour into an 8-ounce glass filled with ice.

Yields 1 drink.

Note: This is a strong drink. For brunch, you may wish to increase the quantity of orange juice. Some mixers like to add a splash of soda water.

Raspberry Cocktail

1 cup fresh raspberries
6 ounces gin
½ ounce kirsch

8 ounces dry white wine
6 fresh raspberries

Mash the raspberries lightly in a bowl. Pour on the gin and let macerate for 2 hours. Strain, pressing on the raspberry pulp to extract the juices. Put the raspberry juice into a blender with the kirsch, wine, and 8 ice cubes. Blend until the ice is crushed. Pour into cocktail glasses and add a fresh raspberry to each glass.

Yields 6 drinks.

Rickeys

Rickeys are similar to fizzes, but are mixed instead of blended.

3 ounces gin, rum, bourbon, or
  Calvados
1 ounce lime juice

½ ounce lemon juice
soda water
1 slice lime

In an 8-ounce glass, place 3 ice cubes. Add the liquor, lime juice, and lemon juice. Stir well and add soda to fill the glass. Garnish with lime slice.

Yields 1 drink.

Singapore Sling

3 ounces gin
½ ounce Cherry Heering
½ ounce lemon juice

water or soda water
1 orange slice

Place 2 or 3 ice cubes in an 8-ounce glass. Add the gin, Cherry Heering, and lemon juice. Fill with water or soda water. Garnish with orange slice.

Yields 1 drink.

Daiquiri

---

3 ounces light rum
¾ ounce lime juice

1 teaspoon confectioners' sugar
1 teaspoon Cointreau

In a blender, combine rum, lime juice, sugar, and Cointreau. Add 1 ice cube and blend until smooth. Pour into a 6-ounce glass.
Yields 1 drink.

FROZEN DAIQUIRI   Add 1 cup of crushed ice to the Daiquiri recipe and blend until mushy.

FRUIT DAIQUIRI   Add ½ fresh peach, ½ banana, or ½ cup strawberries to the blender before blending.

Knickerbocker Special

---

2 ounces rum
1 teaspoon Cointreau
1 slice fresh pineapple
1 teaspoon orange juice

1 teaspoon lemon juice
1 teaspoon raspberry syrup
1 pineapple stick

In a blender, combine the rum, Cointreau, pineapple, and orange, lemon, and raspberry juices. Add 2 ice cubes and blend well. Pour into an 8-ounce glass. Garnish with pineapple stick.
Yields 1 drink.

Pineapple Fizz

---

3 ounces light rum
2 tablespoons minced fresh
  pineapple

1 teaspoon confectioners' sugar
3 ounces soda water

In a blender, combine rum, pineapple, and sugar. Blend until almost smooth. Pour into ice-filled, 8-ounce glass and add soda water.
Yields 1 drink.

Rum Flip

3 ounces rum, brandy, port, or sherry   1½ teaspoons confectioners' sugar
1 egg   nutmeg to taste

In a blender, combine the rum, egg, and sugar. Blend well. Pour into an ice-filled, 8-ounce glass. Sprinkle with nutmeg.
Yields 1 drink.

Sunshine

4 ounces orange juice   2 ounces rum

Combine orange juice and rum in a mixing glass. Mix well. Pour into an ice-filled, 8-ounce glass. Garnish with a slice of lime, if desired.
Yields 1 drink.

Bloody Mary

4 ounces chilled tomato juice   2 drops Tabasco sauce
3 ounces vodka   black pepper to taste
2 teaspoons lemon juice   celery stick, optional
2 drops Worcestershire sauce

In a large (12-ounce) wine glass, combine tomato juice, vodka, lemon juice, Worcestershire, Tabasco, and black pepper. Mix well. Add 2 or 3 ice cubes and celery stick.
Yields 1 drink.
Note: Bloody Marys can also be made with lime juice, or you can substitute gin, rum, or aquavit for the vodka.

Bull Shot

4 ounces cold, strong beef bouillon   salt and pepper to taste
3 ounces vodka

In an ice-filled mixing glass, combine bouillon and vodka. Season with salt and pepper to taste. Mix well. Strain into a large stemmed wine glass.

(cont.)

The bouillon must be completely free of fat or this will prove an unpleasant drink.

Yields 1 drink.

Salty Dog

4 ounces vodka   ¼ teaspoon confectioners' sugar
3 ounces grapefruit juice

In an ice-filled mixing glass, combine vodka, grapefruit juice, and sugar. Mix until the sugar has dissolved. Strain into an 8-ounce wine glass and add an ice cube.

Yields 1 drink.

De Rigueur

2 ounces scotch   1 ounce honey
1 ounce grapefruit juice

In a blender, combine scotch, grapefruit juice, and honey. Add 2 ice cubes and blend well. Pour into an old-fashioned glass.

Yields 1 drink.

Whiskey Sour

3 ounces whiskey, gin, brandy,   1 teaspoon confectioners' sugar
  rum, or Calvados   1 maraschino cherry
1 ounce lemon juice   1 slice orange

In a blender, combine the whiskey, lemon juice, sugar, and 3 ice cubes. Blend until mixed; the ice will be chunky. Strain into a stemmed glass and add the cherry and orange slice.

Yields 1 drink.

Ward 8

3 ounces bourbon
1 ounce lemon juice
1/2 ounce grenadine

soda water
1 orange slice

In a blender, combine the bourbon, lemon juice, grenadine, and 3 ice cubes. Blend until mixed; the ice will be chunky. Strain into a large wine glass. Fill with club soda and garnish with the orange slice.
Yields 1 drink.

Brandy Alexander

2 ounces brandy
1 ounce creme de cacao

1 ounce heavy cream

In a blender, combine the brandy, creme de cacao, cream, and 3 ice cubes. Blend until mixed; the ice will be chunky. Strain into a 6-ounce glass.
Yields 1 drink.
Note: You can substitute gin or vodka for the brandy.

Breakfast Egg Nog

1/2 cup milk
2 ounces brandy
1 ounce Cointreau

1 whole egg
nutmeg to taste

In a blender, combine the milk, brandy, Cointreau, egg, and 3 ice cubes. Blend until well mixed; the ice will be chunky. Strain into a large, stemmed wine glass. Sprinkle with nutmeg.
Yields 1 drink.

Jack Rose

3 ounces apple jack
1 ounce lemon juice

1/2 teaspoon grenadine

In a blender, combine the apple jack, lemon juice, grenadine, and 3 ice cubes. Blend until well mixed; the ice will be chunky. Strain into a cocktail glass.

Yields 1 drink.

Mimosa or Bucks Fizz

2 ounces chilled orange juice   6 ounces chilled champagne

Pour the orange juice into a 10-ounce glass and add the champagne.
Yields 1 drink.

Vermouth Cassis

3 ounces French vermouth   soda water
1 ounce Creme de Cassis

Fill 10-ounce glass with ice. Add the vermouth and Cassis. Fill with soda.

Yields 1 drink.

Hot Drinks

Hot Buttered Rum

3 ounces rum   1 cup hot milk
1½ teaspoons confectioners' sugar   1 tablespoon butter
1-inch piece cinnamon stick   grated nutmeg to taste

Rinse a 12-ounce mug in very hot water and shake dry. Place rum, sugar, and cinnamon stick into the mug. Stir to dissolve the sugar. Pour in hot milk, top with butter, and sprinkle with nutmeg.

Yields 1 drink.

Irish Coffee

1 teaspoon sugar	1½ ounces Irish whiskey
5 ounces strong hot coffee	2 tablespoons whipped cream

Rinse an 8-ounce stemmed goblet in very hot water. Shake dry. Place the sugar in the glass and add the coffee and whiskey. Stir to dissolve the sugar. Top with whipped cream.

Yields 1 drink.

Hot Toddy

3 ounces rye, bourbon, rum, or brandy	1-inch piece cinnamon stick
1 strip lemon peel	pinch of sugar
1 whole clove	boiling water

Rinse an 8-ounce glass in very hot water. Shake dry. Place the whiskey, lemon peel stuck with the clove, cinnamon stick, and sugar in the glass. Add water to fill the glass.

Yields 1 drink.

Note: You can substitute dark rum for the whiskey to make Grog.

Vin Chaud (Gluhwein)

1 slice lemon	1 cinnamon stick
2 whole cloves	1 cup red wine
2 tablespoons sugar	

Stud the lemon slice with the cloves. Combine with the sugar and cinnamon stick in a nonaluminum saucepan. Cook over moderate heat, stirring, until the sugar has melted. Add the wine and bring just to a boil. Strain into a heated mug.

Yields 1 drink.

CHAPTER 2
Appetizers

Perhaps no meal utilizes those appetizer foods found in gourmet shops as well as brunch. Appetizer stores and delicatessens can provide all the makings of a brunch. Depending on your community, it is often possible to buy smoked salmon, bagels, cream cheese, smoked whitefish, prosciutto, Swiss *Bundenfleisch,* assorted breads, soft cheeses, and sweet rolls. These foods, a pot of coffee, and friends can create a superb brunch.

Depending on the type of brunch you are giving, you may or may not choose to serve appetizers (hors d'oeuvre). If the brunch is later in the day and more of a luncheon, then appetizers are definitely in order. If it is earlier and the meal is truly a breakfast, then you and your guests will probably prefer the meal without any preambles. Of course, that breakfast meal may consist of just appetizer foods.

Appetizers can be simple fish or meat offerings or something more elaborate, such as chicken livers in bacon, cheese pastries, or small puffs with a savory filling. Some people prefer to begin the meal with fruit (see chapter 12). The important point is not to overdo. A few carefully selected appetizers will lead the guests into the meal. Do not expect your guests to eat a surfeit of appetizers and then sit down to a full brunch.

RAW VEGETABLES

Raw vegetables (crudites) are not usually served at breakfast, but they can be used as a light appetizer for a later brunch. Guests can choose to dip the vegetables or not and, of course, the bright cheerful colors of the vegetables are a bonus. When choosing vegetables, select those that are colorful and different. Avoid the usual carrots, cucumbers, and celery and include special vegetables, such as snow peas, Belgian endive, or royal beans.

The dips you choose should be light both in flavor and texture. Those that are highly spiced are too strong for this hour.

Caper Dip

¾ cup sour cream
2 teaspoons capers, crushed
¼ teaspoon crushed dried rosemary

juice of 1 lime
salt and pepper to taste

15

In a bowl, combine the sour cream, capers, rosemary, and lime juice. Correct seasoning with salt and pepper.

Keeps 1 week in the refrigerator.

Yields about 1 cup.

Dill Dip

11 ounces cream cheese, softened
1 cup sour cream
3 ounces stuffed olives, minced
3½ tablespoons minced dill
1 teaspoon minced shallots
½ teaspoon Dijon mustard
⅛ teaspoon crushed garlic

1 dash Worcestershire sauce
pepper to taste
2 dashes Tabasco sauce
juice of 1 lemon
salt to taste
¼ teaspoon paprika

In a bowl, combine the cream cheese, sour cream, olives, dill, shallots, mustard, garlic, Worcestershire, pepper, Tabasco, lemon juice, and salt. Blend until smooth. Correct seasoning. Refrigerate covered for 2 hours or longer. Dust with paprika before serving.

Keeps 4 days in the refrigerator.

Yields 2½ cups.

Sour Cream Dill Sauce

1 cup sour cream
½ cup minced dill

salt and pepper to taste

In a bowl, combine the sour cream and dill. Correct seasoning with salt and pepper.

Keeps 5 days in the refrigerator.

Yields about 1 cup.

Pink Mayonnaise

½ cup mayonnaise
2 tablespoons tomato paste
1 teaspoon lemon juice

salt and pepper to taste
1½ tablespoons minced green or red sweet pepper

In a bowl, combine the mayonnaise, tomato paste, and lemon juice. Correct seasoning with salt and pepper. Fold in the minced pepper.

Keeps 2 days in the refrigerator.

Yields about 1/2 cup.

Yogurt Dipping Sauce

1 cup yogurt
1 shallot, minced
1 tablespoon minced basil
1/2 teaspoon dried chervil

pinch of dry marjoram
dash of Worcestershire sauce
salt and pepper to taste

In a bowl, combine the yogurt, shallots, basil, chervil, marjoram, Worcestershire, salt, and pepper. Mix well.

Keeps 5 days in the refrigerator.

Yields 1 cup.

Tapenade

18 anchovy fillets in oil
20 to 24 soft black olives, pitted
3 to 4 cloves garlic
1/4 cup olive oil
4 ounces tuna fish in oil

28 capers
1 tablespoon Dijon mustard
1/4 cup cognac
dash of lemon juice

In a processor, puree the anchovies, olives, and garlic, adding extra oil if needed. Add the tuna fish, capers, mustard, cognac, and lemon juice. Process with on–off turns to combine.

Keeps 8 days in the refrigerator.

Yields 1 cup.

Smoked Salmon Dip

4 ounces smoked salmon, shredded
1/3 cup heavy cream

black pepper to taste
1 teaspoon capers

In a processor, puree the salmon, cream, pepper, and capers. Put into a bowl and grind some black pepper over the top.

Keeps 24 hours in the refrigerator.

Yields about 1 cup.

Taramasalata

⅓ 8-ounce jar tarama	4 to 5 slices white bread, crusts
1 small onion, grated	removed
1½ cups olive oil	¼ to ½ cup lemon juice

In a processor, combine the tarama and onion. Turn on the machine, add 3 tablespoons olive oil, and process until smooth.

Place bread slices in a bowl, cover with ½ cup water, and let soak 3 minutes. Drain, squeezing out the excess moisture. With the machine running, add the bread, remaining olive oil, and lemon juice alternately until all ingredients have been added.

Keeps 4 to 5 days in the refrigerator. Can be frozen for 1 month.

Yields 2 cups.

Note: Tarama (carp roe) is sold in Greek and Middle Eastern markets.

Chipped Beef Dip

---

8 ounces cream cheese, softened	2 tablespoons horseradish or to taste
8 ounces sour cream	salt and pepper to taste
½ cup minced chipped beef	

In a processor, puree the cream cheese and sour cream. With on–off turns, add the beef, horseradish, salt, and pepper until just mixed. Do not puree.

Yields about 2½ cups.

Keeps 3 days in the refrigerator.

CHEESE

In many countries, cheese *is* breakfast, or a major part of it. We tend to serve cream cheese in the morning, enjoying it plain or topping it with jams or smoked fish. Try serving other cheeses, such as Edam, mimolette (French cheddar), a mild chevre, or Stracchino. One of the many flavorful cheese spreads can be a pleasant addition to brunch.

Bibelkase (Bible Cheese)

2 cups small-curd cottage cheese
½ cup heavy cream
3 cloves garlic, minced

1 tablespoon minced parsley
salt and pepper to taste

Force the cottage cheese through a sieve into a bowl. Beat in the cream, garlic, parsley, salt, and pepper.

Keeps 1 week in the refrigerator.

Yields about 2 cups.

Fromage Berrichon

3 ounces cream cheese
1 package Liederkranz cheese
3 tablespoons heavy cream

4 teaspoons Madeira
½ teaspoon celery seed
1 clove garlic, split

In a processor, puree the cream cheese, Liederkranz, heavy cream, Madeira, and celery seeds. Rub the inside of a 1-cup crock with the garlic and discard the garlic. Pack the cheese into the crock and store, covered, for 24 hours.

Keeps 1 week in the refrigerator.

Yields 1 cup.

Herb Cheese

3 ounces cream cheese, softened
2 tablespoons minced parsley
2 tablespoons minced chives

1 tablespoon heavy cream
salt and pepper to taste

In a bowl, cream the cheese until light and fluffy. Beat in the parsley, chives, cream, salt, and pepper.

Keeps 3 days in the refrigerator.

Yields about ½ cup.

Note: Add 1 tablespoon of tarragon, rosemary, or dill, if desired.

FISH

Smoked Salmon Platter

1 pound smoked salmon
8 ounces cream cheese
6 bagels, split and toasted

1 red onion, thinly sliced
black pepper

Arrange the smoked salmon in the center of a platter around the cream cheese. Arrange the bagels around the outside edge and scatter the onion slices over all. Serve black pepper on the side.

Guests construct their own open-faced sandwich by spreading the bagel with cream cheese, topping it with slices of smoked salmon and onion, and sprinkling liberally with freshly ground black pepper.

The platter can be prepared the night before except for the bagels. Toast bagels just before serving.

Serves 6.

Smoked Fish Platter

Arrange smoked fish from your delicatessen, such as sablefish, whitefish, and salmon, on a platter. Decorate with lemon wedges and surround with slices of pumpernickel and rye breads. Serve horseradish cream on the side.

HORSERADISH CREAM

$2/3$ cup heavy cream
4 tablespoons grated horseradish

salt and pepper to taste

Whip the cream until stiff and fold into the horseradish. Correct seasoning with salt and pepper. Serve with smoked fish platter.

Keeps 3 to 4 hours in the refrigerator.

Yields about $1\frac{1}{2}$ cups.

Codfish Balls

1 cup salt cod, shredded
2 cups diced, peeled potatoes
pinch of white pepper
1 egg

$\frac{1}{2}$ tablespoon butter
oil for deep frying
tomato sauce (see Appendix)

Rinse the fish in cold water, then soak in cold water for 1 hour. Rinse again. In a 3-quart saucepan, combine the fish and potatoes with enough water to cover. Simmer until the potatoes are cooked. Drain. Mash the potatoes and fish in a bowl with a wooden spoon or potato masher. Beat in the pepper, egg, and butter. Cool.

Shape into 6 flat cakes and saute in butter until browned on both sides. Or shape into small balls, about 1 inch in diameter, and deep fry at 375° F. until golden. Serve with tomato sauce.

Can be frozen after deep frying.

Yields 6 large cakes or about 48 small balls.

Brandade de Morue

This wonderful dish from the south of France is usually served as a main course, but it makes a delicious, full-flavored appetizer. Serve it with quantities of sauteed bread triangles.

1 pound salt cod	2 or 3 large garlic cloves
½ cup olive oil	pitted ripe olives, optional
½ cup heavy cream	

Soak the salt cod in cold water for 12 hours or longer, changing the water often. Drain the cod and rinse well. Put the cod into a saucepan, cover with cold water, and bring to a boil. Simmer 1 minute and drain. In separate saucepans, heat the oil and cream until hot but not boiling.

Flake the hot drained fish into a processor, add the garlic cloves, and puree the mixture. With the machine running, pour the hot oil and cream alternately into the mixture and process until smooth. The mixture should be the consistency of thick mayonnaise. Serve warm.

Can be made ahead and reheated.

Yields about 3 cups.

Note: You can substitute 1 pound of fresh poached salmon for the cod. Soaking is not necessary.

Finnan Haddie Toasts

2 tablespoons butter	salt and pepper to taste
2 tablespoons flour	6 slices bread, toasted
⅔ cup light cream	6 tablespoons bread crumbs
1 cup cooked, flaked finnan haddie	2 tablespoons melted butter
½ teaspoon lemon juice	lemon wedges

Preheat the broiler.

In a saucepan, melt the butter, stir in the flour, and cook until bubbly. Stir in the cream and cook until thickened and smooth. Fold in the finnan haddie, lemon juice, salt, and pepper. Cut the toast into 4 triangles each. Spread the fish mixture on toast points. Combine the bread crumbs and melted butter and sprinkle on top of the toast points. Broil until golden. Serve with lemon wedges.

Mixture can be made ahead and even frozen. Do not make toast until shortly before broiling.

Yields 24.

Bird's Nest

1 tablespoon capers, drained	3 tablespoons minced parsley
1 medium onion, minced	½ cup cooked beets, minced
1¼ cups minced herring	1 egg yolk

On a 9-inch platter, arrange the ingredients as follows. Place the capers in the center and surround with onions, herring, parsley, and beets. Place the egg yolk in half its shell in an egg cup at the side of the platter. When ready to serve, pour the egg yolk into the center of the platter and mix all of the ingredients together. Serve with Swedish flatbread or rye bread.

Assemble just before serving.

Yields 2 cups.

Potted Kippers

1 pound kippered herring	pepper to taste
½ cup butter	cayenne pepper to taste
2 tablespoons lemon juice	2 tablespoons melted butter

In a bowl, pour boiling water over the kippers and let stand 5 minutes. Drain and pat dry. Remove and discard skin and bones.

In a processor, puree the fish, ½ cup butter, lemon juice, pepper, and cayenne. Pack into a crock and cover with melted butter, if you wish to store. Serve with toast points.

Keeps 1 week in the refrigerator.

Yields 1½ cups.

Angels on Horseback

12 whole oysters   paprika to taste
salt and pepper to taste   12 thin slices bacon

Preheat oven to 375° F.

Sprinkle each oyster with salt, pepper, and paprika. Wrap in bacon strip and secure with a skewer. Bake on a rack until the bacon is crisp.

Can be prepared for baking the day before.

Yields 12.

Salmon Pate

¼ pound unsalted butter, softened   1 teaspoon salt
1½ cups cooked, flaked salmon   pinch of cayenne
  1 teaspoon grated onion   3 tablespoons minced chives
  1 tablespoon lemon juice

In a processor, puree the butter and salmon. While the machine is running, add the onion, lemon juice, salt, and cayenne. Mix in chives with 2 or 3 on–off turns. Store in a covered container overnight to ripen. Serve with toast points or rye bread.

Keeps 5 days in the refrigerator.

Yields about 2 cups.

Note: You can vary the flavor of this pate by changing the herb. Tarragon, dill, and basil are particularly nice. You also can use one pound of smoked salmon for the fresh salmon, or substitute 1½ cups cooked, peeled shrimp.

Scallops and Prosciutto

1 tablespoon minced garlic,
   optional
juice of 2 limes or 2 lemons
1½ pounds sea scallops, halved
  2 teaspoons salt

pepper to taste
½ teaspoon minced basil
½ pound thinly sliced prosciutto
melted butter

In a bowl, combine the garlic and lime juice. Add the scallops, mix well, and cover. Marinate overnight. Drain and season scallops with salt, pepper, and basil.

Preheat oven to 450° F.

Wrap prosciutto slices around scallops and skewer. Brush with melted butter. Bake until scallops are just cooked, about 8 minutes.

Do not keep longer than overnight.

Yields about 36.

Puree of Smoked Trout

3 smoked trout
⅓ cup heavy cream
juice of ½ lemon

2 tablespoons olive oil
minced radishes, optional

Remove the skin and bones from the trout. In a processor, puree the trout, cream, lemon juice, and olive oil. Serve on melba toast with radishes on the side, if desired.

Keeps 4 days in the refrigerator.

Yields 2 cups.

MEATS

Bacon Pinwheels

12 slices white bread, crusts
   removed

6 ounces cream cheese with chives
½ pound bacon

Preheat oven to 350° F.

Spread the bread slices with the cream cheese, thinning it with a little milk if needed. Roll the bread slices jelly-roll fashion and wrap each roll in bacon. Skewer and cut into bite-size pieces. Bake 15 minutes or until the bacon is crisp, turning often.

Can be prepared for baking 2 days before.

Yields 24 pieces.

Note: For variety, use plain cream cheese mixed with 2 tablespoons minced mango chutney, or 1 tablespoon bitter orange marmalade and 1 teaspoon dry mustard.

Grilled Figs and Bacon

12 fresh figs   12 bacon slices

Preheat broiler.

Cut figs into quarters, wrap each quarter in bacon, and skewer. Broil until bacon is cooked.

Can be prepared the day before.

Yields 48 pieces.

Note: Prosciutto can be used instead of the bacon; apricots or chicken livers can be used for the figs.

Swiss, Bacon, and Mushroom Toasts

2½ cups grated Gruyere cheese   2 tablespoons lemon juice
⅔ cup heavy cream   12 slices bacon, cooked
12 slices white bread, crusts   4 eggs
   removed   ⅔ cup milk
12 mushrooms, thinly sliced   ½ cup butter
 2 tablespoons butter

Mix the cheese and cream and spread on the bread slices. Saute the mushrooms in 2 tablespoons butter with the lemon juice. Put 2 slices of bacon and 1 to 2 tablespoons mushrooms on each of 6 slices of cheese-covered bread. Put another slice of bread, cheese side down, on top of the bacon mixture.

Beat the eggs and milk. Dip the sandwiches into the egg mixture. In a 12-inch skillet, heat the butter and saute the sandwiches until browned on both sides. Cut into quarters.

Can be made ahead and reheated in the oven.

Yields 24 pieces.

Smoked Beef with Pears

6 Anjou pears, peeled   ½ pound thinly sliced smoked beef
lemon juice   (*Bundenfleisch*)

Cut the pears into strips and toss with lemon juice. Wrap in beef slices
and skewer.
Serve within a few hours.
Yields about 36.
Note: You can vary this by substituting slices of melon for the pears
or prosciutto for the beef.

Sausage Toasts

¼ pound sausage meat   oil for deep frying
 1 large egg   4 slices white bread, crusts removed
 1 tablespoon minced parsley   minced parsley
½ teaspoon anchovy paste

In a bowl, combine the sausage meat, egg, 1 tablespoon parsley, and
anchovy paste. Mix well.
Heat the oil to 375° F.
Spread the bread slices with sausage mixture, mounding in the center.
Cut into triangles. Fry until golden and cooked through, about 3 minutes.
Sprinkle with parsley.
Can be assembled for frying the day before. Fried toasts can be frozen
and reheated in a 350° F. oven on paper towel-lined sheets until hot.
Yields 16.
Note: For variety, add 1 teaspoon minced gingerroot and omit an-
chovy paste. Or add ¼ teaspoon crushed fennel seeds and a pinch of mar-
joram, omitting the anchovy paste.

APPETIZER PUFFS

Small puffs are delectable appetizers. For the puff recipe, see page 203. Make
the appetizer puffs about the size of a small walnut, 1½ inches in diameter.
You should get between 50 and 75 puffs from the mixture. The puffs can be
made and frozen for up to two months in the freezer.
Any savory filling can be used in the puffs, including many of the recipes already given in this chapter, such as potted kippers, brandade, and
especially the salmon or cheese mixtures.

Cheese Filling for Puffs

3 tablespoons cream cheese	1 tablespoon minced watercress
5 tablespoons butter	1 teaspoon Dijon mustard
1 tablespoon minced parsley	¼ cup ground ham
1 tablespoon minced chives	salt and pepper to taste

In a medium bowl, combine the cheese, butter, parsley, chives, watercress, mustard, ham, salt, and pepper. Use to fill puffs. Can also be used as a spread.

Keeps 2 days in the refrigerator.

Fills about 30 cocktail puffs.

Deviled Chicken Stuffing

2 cups minced chicken	1 tablespoon minced dill
1 cup minced ham	pinch of cayenne
½ cup butter	4 teaspoons minced gherkins
1 tablespoon Dijon mustard	salt and pepper to taste

In a medium bowl, combine the chicken, ham, and butter. Beat until fluffy. Beat in the mustard, dill, cayenne, gherkins, salt, and pepper.

Fills about 50 puffs.

STRUDEL OR PHYLLO APPETIZERS

This paper-thin pastry is available in Middle Eastern stores and many supermarkets. It may be in the frozen food section and it may be spelled differently (filo or fillo).

The pastry is easy to handle if you follow a few simple steps. When ready to work with the pastry, unwrap it and lay it on a flat surface. Cover it with a sheet of waxed paper and a towel that has been wrung out in cold water and is only slightly damp. Remove one sheet of pastry at a time and lay it on a work surface. Brush with butter. If the pastry is *very* thin, it may be necessary to use two sheets together, both buttered.

Shaping Phyllo Dough

ROLLS   Spread the filling in a row along one long edge of the pastry. Fold in the sides about 2 inches and roll as a jelly roll to form a log. Place on a baking sheet and spread with melted butter. Make crosswise cuts halfway through the pastry about an inch apart before baking.

SMALL LOGS   Use 1 sheet of pastry, brush with butter, and cut into 3-inch wide strips. Put a generous teaspoon of filling at one end and fold in the edges ½ inch. Roll the length of the pastry like a jelly roll. Place on baking sheet and brush with melted butter. You can also make a large log by stacking 2 or 3 sheets of buttered phyllo. Bake at 400° F. for about 35 minutes.

TRIANGLES   Use 1 sheet of phyllo, brush with butter, and cut into 3-inch wide strips. Place a generous teaspoon of filling at one end of the pastry. Pick up one corner and fold it over the filling so the short edge aligns with one of the long edges to form a triangle. Pick up the uppermost point and fold it straight down to keep the triangular shape. Continue until you have reached the end of the strip. Place seam side down on a baking sheet and brush with melted butter.

Crab Filling for Phyllo

½ pound crabmeat	½ to ¾ cup Bechamel (see
1 cup minced mushrooms, sauteed	Appendix)
in 1 tablespoon butter until dry	salt and pepper to taste

Preheat oven to 400° F.

In a medium bowl, combine the crabmeat, mushrooms, and enough Bechamel to bind. Correct seasoning with salt and pepper. Fill pastry and bake for 20 minutes or until puffed and golden.

Yields enough filling for 24 pastries. Can be used to fill puffs.

Can be frozen.

Sausage Mushroom Strudel

2 pounds Italian sweet sausage,	salt and pepper to taste
peeled	1 pound ricotta cheese
2 pounds mushrooms, minced	1 pound phyllo
¼ cup minced shallots	1½ cups melted butter
6 tablespoons butter	

Preheat oven to 400° F.

Crumble the sausage meat into a 12-inch skillet and cook, stirring and breaking it into bits, until no longer pink. Set aside.

In the corner of a kitchen towel, squeeze the excess moisture from the mushrooms, a handful at a time. Saute the mushrooms and shallots in butter until the liquid has evaporated. Correct seasoning with salt and pepper. Combine the mushrooms with the sausage and stir in the cheese. Correct seasonings and mix well. Fill pastry and bake for 20 minutes or until puffed and golden.

Can be frozen after baking.

Yields enough filling for about 100 pastries.

Note: You can substitute cream cheese, cottage cheese, or crumbled chevre for the ricotta. For another variation, use ½ pound blue cheese and ½ pound ricotta.

CRACKERS AND BISCUITS

Sesame Seed Cheese Crackers

½ pound grated cheddar cheese	½ teaspoon salt
6 tablespoons butter	1 cup flour
3 tablespoons water	1 teaspoon baking powder
2 tablespoons sesame seeds	1 egg, lightly beaten
1 teaspoon dry mustard	½ teaspoon salt
1 teaspoon Tabasco sauce	sesame seeds

Preheat oven to 350° F.

In a bowl, combine the cheese, butter, water, 2 tablespoons sesame seeds, mustard, Tabasco, and salt. Blend well. Add flour and baking powder and mix until well blended. Wrap in waxed paper and chill 30 minutes.

Butter 2 baking sheets and sprinkle with cold water. Divide dough in half and roll ¼-inch thick. Cut into 1-inch circles. Place on baking sheet. Combine the egg and salt and brush tops of crackers. Sprinkle with sesame seeds. Bake until golden, about 15 minutes.

Can be frozen.

Yields about 40 crackers.

Hot Cheese Balls

¼ pound cheddar or Edam cheese, grated	½ cup sifted flour
	pinch of salt
¼ cup butter	1½ tablespoons sesame, caraway,
1 tablespoon bacon fat	or cumin seeds
pinch of cayenne	

Preheat oven to 450° F.

In a bowl, blend the cheese, butter, bacon fat, cayenne, flour, and salt. Mix well. Mix in sesame seeds. Chill 3 hours.

Roll into 1-inch balls and place on ungreased baking sheet. Bake 15 minutes. Serve hot.

Can be frozen and reheated.

Yields about 36.

Cheese Thins

1 cup sifted flour	2 tablespoons grated Parmesan
1/2 teaspoon salt	cheese
1/4 teaspoon paprika	1/4 cup cold beer
pinch of cayenne	1 egg yolk
3/4 cup grated sharp cheddar cheese	2 tablespoons beer
6 tablespoons butter	caraway or poppy seeds

Preheat oven to 450° F.

In a bowl, combine the flour, salt, paprika, and cayenne. Mix well. Add the cheddar, butter, and Parmesan and blend well. Add the 1/4 cup beer and mix until it forms a dough. Shape the dough on a sheet of waxed paper into a roll 1 inch in diameter. Wrap tightly and freeze until firm.

Slice 1/8-inch thick rounds and arrange on a buttered baking sheet. Combine the egg yolk and remaining beer and brush the top of each round. Sprinkle with caraway or poppy seeds. Bake 12 to 14 minutes or until lightly golden.

Can be frozen.

Yields 60.

Herb Parmesan Biscuits

1 1/4 cups grated Parmesan cheese	3/4 teaspoon oregano
1 cup flour	3/4 teaspoon basil
1/2 cup butter	1/2 teaspoon Worcestershire sauce
3/4 teaspoon marjoram	2 to 3 tablespoons white wine

Preheat oven to 400° F.

In a bowl, combine the cheese, flour, butter, and herbs. Blend until the mixture resembles coarse meal. Stir in the Worcestershire and wine to form a dough. Shape into a log 1½ inches in diameter, wrap in waxed paper, and chill until firm.

Slice log into ¼-inch slices and arrange ½ inch apart on lightly buttered baking sheets. Bake 12 to 15 minutes or until lightly browned.

Can be frozen.

Yields 48.

CHAPTER 3
Eggs

If any single food signifies breakfast and brunch it is the egg. Certainly no other food is as versatile. The egg can be sauteed, poached, broiled, baked, steamed, deep fried, separated, or emulsified. It is delicious sour or sweet, hot or cold, firm or soft. Furthermore, the egg is nutritionally sound and inexpensive.

Eggs contain protein, which hardens in heat. Therefore, eggs must be treated gently, for instance, soft cooked not boiled. It only takes a short time for eggs to cook, but cooks often want to rush them. The one egg recipe that requires intense heat is the omelet, but the omelet must be cooked quickly before the eggs have a chance to toughen. Treat eggs with respect and you will be rewarded with superlative dishes.

As simple as it is to cook eggs, they are often prepared poorly. Some methods are unnecessarily complicated, others are not detailed enough. The number of eggs you serve to one person depends on the contents of the rest of the meal and the size of the eggs. If the menu is principally the egg dish, use two large eggs per person. If several foods are on the menu, then two medium eggs are sufficient. If the menu is abundant, one large egg will suffice.

PRESENTATION

Traditionally, many egg dishes are served individually. However, most recipes look more impressive, and are easier and quicker to serve, in a large platter or baking dish.

SAUCES

Eggs lend themselves to sauces. The recipes in this chapter incorporate a number of sauces. Sauces that are used more than once in the book have been included in the Appendix for easy reference.

Sauce preparation may at first seem difficult and confusing but it is not. Many sauces can be prepared ahead, frozen, and reheated. Even for those that require some last-minute preparation, there are instructions on preparations that can be done ahead, and directions on how to avoid or, if necessary, correct the pitfalls.

It is important that you use correct recipes with the required ingredients. Eggs Benedict is made with English muffins, Canadian bacon, poached eggs, and Hollandaise sauce, not with toast, ham or bacon, poached eggs, and heated mayonnaise. Oleomargarine is not a substitute for butter. If you cannot use the proper ingredients, then select another dish to prepare.

POACHED EGGS

Poached eggs are perhaps the supreme brunch dish, with Eggs Benedict the *ne plus ultra*. Perfectly poached eggs are easy to prepare and can be made ahead. There are numerous ways to poach eggs, some of which are more humorous than practical. Poached eggs must be made from the freshest eggs if the white is to stay firmly around the yolk. To judge the freshness, crack the shell and slip the egg into a saucer. Look at it carefully. The yolk should stand high, the white should be viscous and cling to the yolk, and there should be a minimum amount of watery liquid at the edges of the white. As an egg loses its freshness, the yolk flattens and the white becomes more watery. Ideally for poaching, you want freshly laid eggs. However, since you do not always know the age of the eggs, you can help the whites to coagulate around the yolks when poaching by adding 1 tablespoon of distilled vinegar to each quart of salted water.

To Poach Eggs

In a large skillet, heat to 185° F. enough salted, vinegared water to float the eggs. If you do not have a thermometer look at the bubbles of water in the skillet. They should be tiny and break just below the surface, like the bubbles in a glass of champagne.

When the water is ready, break the egg into a saucer or cup. Traditionally, this was done to check for rotten eggs; the reason now is to make sure that you have not broken the yolk. If it is broken, set it aside for another use. Place the edge of the saucer so it is touching the water and slide in the egg. Let it poach for 3 to 5 minutes or until done to your taste. Use a slotted spoon to remove the egg and drain well.

Another method of poaching eggs is to put the water in a saucepan and bring it to the correct temperature. With a spoon, swirl the water to make a whirlpool and slip the egg from the saucer into the whirlpool. The whirlpool will keep the white around the yolk.

You can also mold perfectly shaped eggs. Heat the water in a skillet to the correct temperature. Place a French poached egg stand in the water and break the egg into it. You can also use a cookie cutter or other open ring-like form to contain the egg. It is possible to make any shape depending on the cutter. Children will enjoy egg rabbits at Easter or stars at Christmas. Once the eggs have been poached, remove them with a slotted spoon, drain well, and trim the edges, if necessary. Garnish as desired.

Note: Poached eggs are poached in a liquid. Eggs cooked in pans or cups, surrounded by liquid, are coddled.

If you plan to serve a large number of people, it is possible to poach the eggs as early as the night before. Poach them slightly less than you would normally. Remove them from the poaching liquid to a bowl of cold water to stop the cooking. Refrigerate the eggs in the cold water until ready to use. Pour off the cold water and *gently* pour hot, not boiling, water over the eggs. Change the water as often as required until the eggs are hot. Drain and serve.

Eggs Benedict *New Year's Day = Jan 2005 GREAT! & EASY!*

6 English muffins, split and toasted
12 thin slices Canadian bacon, broiled

12 poached eggs, drained
¾ cup Hollandaise sauce *Knorr Pkgd. or pg. 116, 117*
black olive or truffle cutouts, optional *omit.*

Arrange two muffin halves on each plate, top with Canadian bacon slices, place a poached egg on top of each, and coat with the Hollandaise. Garnish with black olive or truffle cutouts, if desired. Serve immediately.

Serves 6.

Asparagus and Mushrooms with Poached Eggs and Hollandaise Sauce

½ pound mushrooms, thinly sliced
1 cup Bechamel sauce
6 English muffins, split and toasted

1 pound asparagus, cooked
butter
6 poached eggs
¾ cup Hollandaise sauce

In a saucepan, combine the mushrooms and Bechamel and heat until almost boiling. Place an English muffin half on each of 6 plates, or on a large platter. Arrange the asparagus on the muffins and coat with mushroom sauce. Spread remaining muffins with butter, top with poached eggs, and coat with Hollandaise. Arrange on the plates or platter.

The mushroom sauce can be made up to 24 hours before serving. The eggs can be poached and the asparagus cooked the night before. Do not toast the muffins or prepare the Hollandaise the day before.

Serves 6.

Eggs Brookside

3 cups pureed spinach (see   2 tablespoons butter
   Appendix)   6 poached eggs
6 slices of ham, 3 inches in   ¾ cup Hollandaise sauce
   diameter   1 teaspoon tarragon

Arrange the puree on a serving plate. Saute the ham slices in butter
until heated and place on spinach. Top each with a poached egg. Combine
the Hollandaise and tarragon and coat the eggs. Assemble just before serving.
   Serves 6.

Eggs California

2 10-ounce packages frozen arti-   12 poached eggs
   choke hearts   1 cup Hollandaise sauce
6 tablespoons butter

Cook the artichokes according to package directions until tender. Drain
and chop. Reheat the artichokes in butter and arrange them on 6 serving plates.
Place poached eggs on the artichokes and coat with the sauce.
   Artichokes and eggs can be prepared the night before.
   Serves 6.

Oeufs Poches a la Crecy
(Poached Eggs with Carrot Puree)

3 cups carrot puree (see Appendix)   1 cup Mousseline sauce (see
6 poached eggs   Appendix)

Preheat broiler.
   Spread the carrot puree evenly in an 8 by 11 baking dish. Arrange
eggs on top, coat with the sauce, and glaze under the broiler until golden.
Serve immediately.
   The eggs and puree can be prepared the night before.
   Serves 6.

Oeufs Poches au Saumon Fume
(Poached Eggs with Smoked Salmon)

2 tablespoons butter
6 English muffins, split and
  toasted
12 slices smoked salmon, at room
  temperature

12 poached eggs
¾ cup Hollandaise sauce

Butter the muffins and arrange on 6 plates. Place a slice of salmon on each muffin, top with the eggs, and coat with sauce.

Eggs can be prepared the night before.

Serves 6.

Oeufs Poches a la Bearnaise
(Poached Eggs with Bearnaise Sauce)

2½ pounds potatoes, peeled
6 tablespoons butter
½ cup milk
salt and pepper to taste

¼ pound butter, melted
12 poached eggs
¾ cup Bearnaise sauce

Preheat oven to 450° F.

Boil the potatoes in water to cover until tender. Drain and dry over heat. Rice the potatoes into a bowl, and beat in the 6 tablespoons butter and milk to form a smooth puree. Season.

On a well-buttered baking sheet, form the potatoes into six large nests using a 16-inch pastry bag with a #5 open star tip. Bake until golden brown and heated through, about 5 minutes.

Carefully transfer the nests to serving dishes, fill with poached eggs, and coat with sauce.

Best when freshly made, but potatoes can be shaped, covered, and refrigerated and eggs poached the night before.

Serves 6.

Poached Eggs Borgia

6 large, firm tomatoes
salt and pepper to taste

12 poached eggs
1 cup Bearnaise sauce

Preheat oven 350° F.

Cut the tomatoes in half and sprinkle with salt and pepper. Place in a baking dish and bake 12 to 15 minutes, or until very hot. Arrange the eggs on the tomatoes and coat with sauce. Can be served on individual plates or from the baking dish.

Eggs can be poached the night before.

Serves 6.

Oeufs Poches Henri IV (Poached Eggs Henry the Fourth)

12 poached eggs   1½ cups Bearnaise sauce
  6 croustades (see Appendix)

Preheat broiler.

Place the poached eggs on the croustades and coat with Bearnaise. Glaze under the broiler until golden.

Eggs can be poached the night before.

Serves 6.

Oeufs Poches Jenny Lind (Poached Eggs Jenny Lind)

  6 sauteed croutons (see   6 poached eggs
    Appendix)   ¾ cup Bearnaise sauce
1½ cups cauliflower puree (see
    Appendix)

Spread the croutons with the cauliflower puree and top with poached eggs. Coat eggs with the sauce.

The puree and the eggs can be made the night before. Reheat before serving.

Serves 6.

Eggs Massena

12 cooked artichoke bottoms   ¾ cup tomato sauce (see Appendix)
¾ cup Bearnaise sauce   12 slices poached marrow
12 poached eggs   minced parsley

Arrange the artichoke bottoms on a plate, coat with Bearnaise, and place one egg on top of each. Coat with tomato sauce and garnish with a slice of marrow and a sprinkling of parsley. Serve immediately.

The artichokes, eggs, and tomato sauce can be prepared ahead. Serves 6.

ARTICHOKE BOTTOMS With a sharp knife, trim the base and upper leaves of the artichoke, exposing the flesh. Dip into acidulated water often during the trimming. Cut out the thistle-like center of the bottom and discard. Poach artichoke bottoms in acidulated water until tender. They can be prepared two days ahead.

BONE MARROW Place the marrow bones in salted boiling water and barely simmer for 10 minutes. Remove the bones from the water, cool a few minutes, and carefully remove the marrow. Cool. Cut into slices.

Oeufs Poches Aurore (Poached Eggs Aurora)

12 croutons (see Appendix)
12 poached eggs
salt and pepper to taste
3 cups Bechamel sauce

¾ cup tomato sauce (see Appendix)
4 hard-cooked egg yolks, sieved

Arrange the croutons on 6 serving plates and top with eggs. Season with salt and pepper. In a small saucepan, combine the Bechamel and tomato puree and heat. Coat each egg with the sauce. Sprinkle eggs with the sieved yolks.
Serves 6.

Oeufs Poches a la Florentine (Poached Eggs Florentine)

1½ pounds wilted spinach
1½ cups Mornay sauce
12 poached eggs

6 tablespoons grated Gruyere or Parmesan cheese
6 tablespoons buttered bread crumbs

Preheat the broiler.

Squeeze the spinach dry and chop finely. Mix the spinach with ¾ cup Mornay sauce. Spread the spinach puree in the bottom of 6 individual baking dishes or 1 large baking dish. Arrange the eggs on top and coat with the remaining sauce. Sprinkle with cheese and bread crumbs. Brown under the broiler.

Can be assembled the night before and refrigerated. Let come to room temperature before baking at 350° F. until golden and bubbling hot. If necessary, brown under the broiler. Do not reheat too long or the eggs will be hard cooked.

Serves 6.

Oeufs Poches Beatrice (Poached Eggs Beatrice)

6 hot poached eggs	3 tablespoons grated Parmesan
6 croutons	cheese
1 cup Mornay sauce	18 spears hot cooked asparagus
½ cup minced cooked mushrooms	3 cups tomato sauce

Preheat broiler.

Place eggs on the croutons in individual ovenproof dishes or a large baking dish. Combine the Mornay sauce with the mushrooms and coat the eggs. Sprinkle with the cheese and broil until golden brown.

Arrange asparagus around the eggs and pour the tomato sauce around the edges. Serve at once.

Eggs and sauce can be prepared the night before.

Serves 6.

Oeufs Poches a la Portugaise (Poached Eggs Portuguese)

4½ cups hot cooked rice	salt and pepper to taste
½ cup hot tomato puree	1½ cups hot Mornay sauce
12 poached eggs	1½ cups grated Gruyere cheese

Preheat the broiler.

Combine the rice and tomato puree and spread in the bottom of a large ovenproof serving dish. Arrange eggs on top and season with salt and pepper. Coat eggs with Mornay sauce and sprinkle with cheese. Glaze under broiler.

Can be prepared for baking the night before. Let come to room temperature before baking at 350° F. until golden brown and bubbling.

Serves 6.

Oeufs Poches a la Hongroise (Poached Eggs Hungarian)

1 green pepper
2 tomatoes, peeled, seeded, and
    chopped
3 large onions, diced
3 tablespoons butter
½ teaspoon caraway seeds

¾ cup heavy cream
1 tablespoon paprika
salt and pepper to taste
½ cup sour cream
6 poached eggs
6 large croutons

Put the pepper in boiling water to cover and simmer 12 minutes. Drain, peel, and cut into ¼ inch dice. Saute the pepper, tomatoes, and onions in butter for 5 minutes. Add the caraway seeds and simmer until tender. Add heavy cream, paprika, and salt and pepper to taste. Without bringing to a boil, stir in the sour cream. Correct seasoning with salt and pepper. On a serving plate, place a poached egg on a crouton and coat with sauce.

Sauce and eggs can be prepared ahead and reheated gently.

Serves 6.

Oeufs Poches a l'Andalouse (Poached Eggs Andalusian)

6 sweet green peppers, blanched
6 cups rice pilaf (see following
    recipe)
12 chicken livers, sauteed, sliced

12 poached eggs
¾ cup tomato sauce (see
    Appendix)

Halve peppers lengthwise, remove seeds, and fill with pilaf. Arrange chicken liver slices on the rice and top with the eggs. Coat with sauce.

The rice-filled peppers can be prepared ahead and reheated in a 350° F. oven, covered, until hot.

Serves 6.

RICE PILAF

3 cups tomato sauce (see
    Appendix)
3 cups chicken or beef stock

salt and pepper to taste
3 cups uncooked long grain rice
3 tablespoons butter, softened

In a heavy 3-quart saucepan or casserole, bring the tomato sauce and beef stock to a boil. Season with salt and pepper to taste.

Pour in the rice; stir until it returns to a boil. Lower the heat and cover tightly. Simmer 20 minutes or until the liquid has been absorbed and the rice is tender, but still resistant to the bite. Gently fold in the butter with a fork.

Poached Eggs with Anchovy Toast and Grilled Tomatoes

2 ounces anchovy fillets, mashed
7 tablespoons butter, softened
6 slices bread, toasted
6 tomatoes, cut in half

2 tablespoons minced basil or
  parsley
12 poached eggs
salt and pepper to taste

In a bowl, cream the anchovies and 4 tablespoons butter until light and fluffy. Spread on toast. Dot tomatoes with remaining butter and sprinkle with the basil or parsley. Broil 5 minutes.

Arrange toasts and tomato on a platter. Place eggs on toast, season, and serve.

Anchovy butter and eggs can be prepared the night before.
Serves 6.

Tschimbur (Poached Eggs with Garlic Yogurt Sauce)

3 cups yogurt
3 cloves garlic, crushed
salt and pepper to taste

12 poached eggs
½ cup butter
3 tablespoons paprika

In a 1-quart saucepan, warm the yogurt with the garlic, salt, and pepper. Arrange eggs on 6 serving plates and coat with the sauce. Heat the butter in a small saucepan with the paprika until fragrant. Pour over the eggs and serve.

Eggs can be prepared the night before.
Serves 6.

Oeufs Poches a la Haut Brion (Poached Eggs in Red Wine)

2 leeks, julienne
2 tablespoons butter
3 cups red wine, preferably bordeaux
salt, pepper, and nutmeg to taste
1 bouquet garni (thyme, bay leaf,
  parsley) (see Glossary)

1 tablespoon beurre manie (see
  Glossary)
6 potato cakes
6 slices ham, same size as potato
  cakes
6 poached eggs

In a skillet, saute the leeks in the butter until tender. Add the wine, salt, pepper, nutmeg, and bouquet garni and simmer 30 minutes. Strain, reserving the liquid.

In a medium-size saucepan, stir the beurre manie into the simmering liquid until it is thickened. Arrange potato cakes on a plate, top with ham eggs, and sauce. Serve.

The sauce can be made ahead and frozen. The potato cakes can be prepared for sauteing the day before.

Serves 6.

POTATO CAKES   Shape the potato mixture from the Poached Eggs with Bearnaise Sauce recipe (page 37) into cakes about 3 inches across and ½ inch thick. Saute in 6 tablespoons butter until golden on both sides.

Cold Poached Eggs

Although not well known, some of the most delicious poached egg dishes are served cold. The small selection included here would be perfect for summer brunch, or even a spring or fall luncheon.

Oeufs aux Crevettes (Cold Poached Eggs with Shrimp)

6 cold poached eggs, trimmed	¾ cup heavy cream, whipped
½ pound small shrimp, cooked, peeled, and deveined	salt and pepper to taste
¾ cup mayonnaise	3 tablespoons minced chives, or dill

Place the eggs in a serving dish. Surround with the shrimp. Fold the mayonnaise and cream together and correct the seasoning with salt and pepper. Coat the eggs with the sauce and sprinkle with chives or dill.

The eggs and sauce can be made the day before. Do not assemble until shortly before serving.

Serves 6.

Oeufs Poches au Cari Mayonnaise
(Poached Eggs with Curry Mayonnaise)

6 cold poached eggs, trimmed	mango chutney
curry powder to taste	chopped salted cashews
1 cup mayonnaise	toasted coconut
1 sieved, hard cooked egg	

Arrange eggs in a serving dish. In a small bowl, combine the curry powder and mayonnaise and spoon over the eggs. Serve the sieved egg, chutney, cashews, and coconut separately in small bowls.

Can be prepared for serving the day before.

Serves 6.

Oeufs Poches Tartare (Poached Eggs Tartar)

3 medium tomatoes, halved	6 cold poached eggs, trimmed
salt and pepper to taste	2 tablespoons minced parsley
2 cups cold, cooked mixed	2 tablespoons minced gherkins
vegetables	lettuce
1 cup mayonnaise	

Scoop out the center of the tomatoes and dice the pulp. Season the tomato shell with salt and pepper. Combine the minced pulp with the mixed vegetables (potatoes, carrots, and green beans cut into ¼ inch dice, and peas are traditional) and ¼ cup mayonnaise.

Fill the tomato shells with the vegetables and top with poached eggs. Coat eggs with remaining mayonnaise. Sprinkle with parsley and gherkins. Serve on a bed of lettuce.

Can be prepared the day before. Refrigerate covered.

Serves 6.

Oeufs Poches Virginia Club (Poached Eggs Virginia Club)

2 cups cooked corn kernels	watercress
⅔ cup mayonnaise	3 medium tomatoes, quartered
salt and pepper to taste	olive oil
6 cold poached eggs, trimmed	black olives

In a small bowl, combine the corn with ¼ cup mayonnaise and salt and pepper to taste. Shape the corn mixture into a base on a serving platter. Chill.

Coat the eggs with the remaining mayonnaise and arrange on top of the corn. Garnish the platter with watercress and tomatoes seasoned with salt, pepper, and olive oil. Decorate with black olives.

Can be arranged the night before, but let it come to room temperature before serving.

Serves 6.

HARD- AND SOFT-COOKED EGGS

Because eggs must be treated gently, boiling them can be a mistake. If you boil them rapidly for an extended time, they become tough, rubbery, and indigestible. If you treat them gently, you will be rewarded with firm tender whites and properly cooked yolks, and hard-cooked eggs will have no unsightly green ring.

To Soft Cook Eggs

Place the eggs in a saucepan large enough to hold them comfortably with 1 inch of water above the top egg. Remove the eggs from the pan and place it and the water over high heat. Bring to a full rolling boil. Gently lower the eggs into the pan with a metal basket or slotted spoon. Cover the pan and let the eggs sit in the water, off the heat, for 6 to 8 minutes, or until they are cooked to the degree desired. Immediately run them under cold water to stop further cooking and to cool the shell for peeling. You will have a fully cooked white with a runny yolk. If it is necessary to reheat the eggs, put them in very hot, not boiling, water until heated through (as with poached eggs). See page 35.

To Hard Cook Eggs

Place the eggs in a pan of cold water with 1 inch of water over the top egg. Leave the eggs in the pan of water, place it over high heat, and bring it rapidly to a boil. Cover the pan, remove it from the heat, and let it stand for 12 minutes. Drain and run the eggs under cold water to prevent further cooking. You will have a fully cooked, tender white and a fully cooked yolk without any green ring. Reheat as for soft-cooked eggs.

Cracked Shells

If you have trouble with shells that crack on hard- or soft-cooked eggs, it is because the shells were already cracked. They may have been cracked when you purchased them, or you may have cracked them when dropping them into the pan of water. Place the eggs in the pan gently. It is possible to hard or soft cook eggs that have been taken from the coldest refrigerator without cracking them, providing they were not cracked beforehand. However, even a hairline fracture of the shell will expand under heat, making a large rift in the shell.

Eggs used for poaching must be as fresh as possible; those used for soft or hard cooking should be a day or two old. Air will then have had a chance to penetrate the shell, making peeling much easier. If there is a large dent at one end when you peel the egg, it was older than desired. Such eggs are not dangerous, they are simply not as pretty.

To Peel Soft- or Hard-Cooked Eggs

Using the back of a spoon or a counter top, gently tap the egg on all sides. Some authors insist that if you let eggs stand in water for a few minutes after cracking the shells, they will be easier to peel. This author has not found a noticeable difference. Gently pry the shell and inner membrane away from the egg. It does help to do this under running water.

Serving Hard- and Soft-Cooked Eggs

Soft-cooked eggs can be eaten directly from the shell set into egg cups, accompanied by freshly made buttered toast; they can also be garnished elaborately. The recipes that call for poached eggs and many of those that call for hard-cooked eggs can also be used with soft-cooked eggs.

Like poached eggs, soft-cooked eggs can be cooked the night before and reheated in the morning. Since peeling is not only tedious but also somewhat dangerous (too much force and the white will split, allowing the yolk to run out), it is advisable to allow plenty of time and to cook a few extra eggs, just in case. If the extra eggs are not needed, you can cook them longer and use them for egg salad or some other recipe.

Hard-cooked eggs can be garnished most elaborately and can be served hot or cold. If you are having a number of guests for brunch, it is wise to cook the eggs and peel them the night before. If some do not peel perfectly, you can cook a few more. Note that not every recipe calls for perfectly peeled eggs. If you have had trouble peeling the eggs and the surface is not perfectly smooth, the garnishes may well hide a multitude of sins. If you do not say anything, only you and the egg will know. Remember that truly fresh eggs are more difficult to peel.

In many of these recipes you will need to reheat the entire preparation in the oven before arranging the dish. In others, the eggs must be heated separately, then sauced and served. Follow the instructions for reheating poached or soft-cooked eggs if the eggs must be reheated.

Oeufs Farcis a la Hollandaise (Stuffed Eggs with Hollandaise)

½ pound mushrooms, minced
2 tablespoons butter
12 hard-cooked eggs, halved
4 tablespoons grated Parmesan
   cheese

1 tablespoon tomato paste
¼ cup heavy cream
1½ cups Hollandaise sauce

Preheat oven to 350° F.

In a 9-inch skillet, saute the mushrooms in the butter until the liquid has evaporated. Remove yolks from eggs and sieve, then stir into the mushrooms along with the cheese, tomato paste, and cream. Stuff the whites with this mixture. (Use a #4 large star tip in a pastry bag to make the job easier and the result prettier.) Arrange eggs in a baking dish and reheat in the oven. Coat with warm Hollandaise just before serving.

Can be prepared for baking the evening before.

Serves 6.

Oeufs Durs Aurore (Hard-Cooked Eggs Aurora)

6 hard-cooked eggs, peeled and
   halved
4 tablespoons butter, softened
1 tablespoon tomato paste

1 cup Bechamel sauce
salt and pepper to taste
½ cup tomato sauce

Preheat oven to 350° F.

Remove yolks from eggs and force through a sieve into a 2-cup bowl. Beat in 2 tablespoons of butter, tomato paste, and ¼ cup Bechamel. Correct seasoning with salt and pepper. Fit a 12-inch pastry bag with a #4 open star tip and stuff the whites. Arrange in a baking dish. Melt remaining butter and pour over the eggs. Reheat in the oven.

In a saucepan, combine the tomato sauce and remaining Bechamel and bring just to a boil. Pour over eggs and serve. Glaze under the broiler, if desired.

Can be assembled the night before, including the sauce, and reheated at 350° F.

Serves 6.

Oeufs Durs a la Bretonne (Hard-Cooked Eggs Brittany)

½ cup minced onions
½ cup minced leeks
½ cup mushrooms
6 tablespoons butter

2 cups hot Bechamel sauce
6 hard-cooked eggs, peeled and
halved

Preheat the broiler.

In separate skillets (or the same skillet in succession), saute the onions, leeks, and mushrooms in 2 tablespoons of butter each until very soft, but not brown. *Do not* saute them together. Combine the vegetables with the Bechamel sauce.

In the bottom of an 8 by 11 baking dish, spoon a layer of the sauce. Arrange the eggs on top, cut side down. If they did not peel perfectly arrange them cut side up. Coat with the remaining sauce. Glaze under the broiler.

This dish can be assembled the night before and reheated at 350° F. until bubbling and lightly browned on top.

Serves 6.

Oeufs Durs a la Sauce Moutarde (Hard-Cooked Eggs with Mustard Sauce)

1 cup Bechamel sauce
1 teaspoon dry mustard, or to taste
salt and pepper to taste

6 hard-cooked eggs, peeled and
halved

Preheat broiler.

In a saucepan, heat the Bechamel and stir in the mustard and salt and pepper to taste. Arrange the eggs in a shallow baking dish and pour the sauce over them. Brown under the broiler.

Can be assembled the night before and reheated at 350° F.

Serves 6.

Note: For a less pungent flavor, substitute Dijon mustard to taste for the dry mustard.

Oeufs a la Tripe, Bourgeoise (Eggs Tripe-Style)

2 large onions, minced
4 tablespoons butter
4 tablespoons flour
1 quart milk, scalded

salt and pepper to taste
nutmeg to taste
12 hard-cooked eggs, peeled and
  quartered

In a 1-quart saucepan, over medium heat, cook the onions in the butter until very soft, but not brown. Sprinkle with flour and cook, stirring until the mixture starts to turn golden. Stir in the milk and cook, stirring, until the mixture comes to a boil and is thickened. Season with salt, pepper, and nutmeg. Simmer gently, stirring often, for 20 minutes. Puree in a processor or blender, or force through a food mill.

Transfer to a clean saucepan and reheat. Arrange the eggs in a serving dish and pour the sauce over them.

Can be prepared the day before and reheated at 350° F.

Serves 6.

Oeufs Farcis a la Chimay (Stuffed Eggs Chimay)

½ cup minced mushrooms
2½ tablespoons butter
6 hard-cooked eggs, halved

1 cup Mornay sauce
salt to taste
1 tablespoon grated Parmesan cheese

Preheat broiler.

In a small skillet, saute the mushrooms in 1 tablespoon butter until tender and the liquid has evaporated. Remove the yolks from the eggs and force through a sieve. Combine the yolks with the remaining butter, mushrooms, ¼ cup Mornay sauce, and salt to taste. Stuff the whites, using a #4 open plain tip if desired.

Place a thin layer of remaining Mornay sauce in the bottom of a baking dish and arrange the eggs on top. Coat with remaining sauce. Sprinkle with cheese and glaze under the broiler.

Can be prepared the day before and reheated at 350° F. Glaze under a broiler if desired.

Serves 6.

Eggs Huntington

1½ cups chicken veloute
  6 hard-cooked eggs, minced
  3 tablespoons grated cheese

3 tablespoons pumpernickel bread
  crumbs

Preheat broiler.

Combine the veloute and eggs. Fill individual buttered ramekins or a 3-cup baking dish. Sprinkle the top with cheese and bread crumbs and glaze under the broiler.

Can be assembled the night before and reheated at 350° F. until hot and delicately browned.

Serves 6.

Oeufs Durs a la Hongroise (Hard-Cooked Eggs Hungarian)

6 hard-cooked eggs, halved
4 tablespoons minced onion
4 tablespoons butter
1 teaspoon paprika

salt and pepper to taste
  3 ripe tomatoes, ½-inch thick slices
lemon juice to taste
½ cup heavy cream

Remove the yolks from the whites and force them through a sieve. In a small skillet, saute the onion in the butter until soft, but not brown. Stir half of the onion mixture into the yolks with ½ teaspoon paprika. Correct seasoning with salt and pepper to taste. Fill egg whites using a 12-inch pastry bag fitted with a #4 large open star tip, if desired.

Saute the tomato slices in the remaining butter-onion mixture until hot and tender. Place tomato slices and onions in a baking dish and arrange eggs on top. Combine the remaining paprika, lemon juice, and cream in the skillet. Bring just to a boil and pour over the eggs. If necessary, reheat at 350° F.

Can be prepared the day before and reheated at 350° F.

Serves 6.

Meulemeester Eggs

6 hard-cooked eggs, chopped
½ pound medium shrimp, cooked,
  peeled, and deveined
1 cup heavy cream
1 teaspoon minced parsley

½ teaspoon Dijon mustard
½ teaspoon minced chervil
salt and pepper to taste
3 tablespoons grated Gruyere cheese
2 tablespoons butter

Preheat the broiler.

In a bowl, combine the eggs, shrimp, cream, parsley, mustard, chervil salt, and pepper. Mix well. Arrange in a buttered baking dish, sprinkle with cheese, and dot with butter. Glaze under the broiler.

Can be prepared for broiling the night before. If necessary reheat at 350° F. before broiling.

Serves 6.

Eggs and Oysters

1 tablespoon minced onion
2 tablespoons butter
4 tablespoons flour
24 shucked oysters and liquor

salt, pepper, and nutmeg to taste
6 hard-cooked eggs, halved
3 cups boiled rice
minced parsley

In a 1-quart saucepan, saute the onion in the butter until soft, but not brown. Stir in the flour and cook the roux until it starts to turn golden.

Poach the oysters in their own liquor until plump and edges just begin to curl. Drain, saving the oysters and the liquor. Add enough water to the oyster liquor to make 2 cups. Add the oyster liquor to the roux and cook, stirring, until thickened and smooth. Simmer 10 minutes. Correct seasoning with salt, pepper, and nutmeg.

Fold the eggs and oysters into the sauce and heat gently. Serve over rice and sprinkle with parsley.

Sauce can be prepared the day before and reheated.

Serves 6.

Oeufs Durs Mistral (Hard-Cooked Eggs Mistral)

6 cold hard-cooked eggs, halved
salt and pepper to taste
1 cup mayonnaise
6 ½-inch thick tomato slices

6 pimiento stuffed olives, halved
  lengthwise
½ cup imported ripe olives
2 parsley sprigs

Sprinkle the cut sides of the eggs with salt and pepper. Coat the rounded sides with mayonnaise and place the eggs, cut side down, on tomato slices. Arrange on a serving dish and top each egg with an olive half, cut side up. Garnish with black olives and parsley sprigs.

For the freshest, prettiest appearance prepare no more than 2 hours before serving.

Serves 6.

Cold Hard-Cooked Eggs with Skordalia (Garlic Mayonnaise)

6 cold hard-cooked eggs, halved
3 tomatoes, quartered
½ cup sun-cured black olives
18 small radishes
4 large garlic cloves
yolk of 1 egg

salt and pepper to taste
lemon juice to taste
½ cup olive oil
¼ cup fresh white bread crumbs
¼ cup ground almonds
minced parsley

Arrange eggs, tomatoes, olives, and radishes on 6 serving plates.

In a processor or blender, puree the garlic. Add egg yolk, salt, pepper, and 2 teaspoons lemon juice. Turn the machine on and add oil as for mayonnaise. Process until thickened. With the machine running, add the bread crumbs, almonds, and parsley. Correct seasoning with lemon juice, salt, and pepper. Drizzle some of the sauce over the eggs and serve the remainder separately.

Sauce can be made ahead. Keeps for 3 days in the refrigerator.

Serves 6.

Oeufs a la Mozart (Cold Hard-Cooked Eggs Mozart)

8 hard-cooked eggs
anchovy paste to taste
2½ cups mayonnaise (see Appendix)

6 gherkins, or spiced cherries
3 tablespoons minced chives
3 tomatoes, peeled, halved, and
  hollowed

Cut two eggs in half and force the whites through a sieve. Cut one quarter out of each remaining egg and remove the yolks. Force all of the yolks through a sieve into a bowl. Beat in the anchovy paste to taste and just enough mayonnaise to bind. Pipe the mixture into the whites using a 12-inch pastry bag fitted with a #4 open star tip. Decorate the yolk with gherkins or cherries and sprinkle with the chives. Arrange cut side up in the tomato shells.

Sieve the remaining sections of whites and combine with the already sieved whites. Sprinkle over the remaining mayonnaise and serve separately.

Can be prepared the day before.

Serves 6.

Oeufs a la Parisienne (Hard-Cooked Eggs Parisian)

6 hard-cooked eggs, halved
6 tablespoons butter
1 tablespoon minced chives
salt and pepper to taste
6 peeled tomatoes, halved
sugar to taste
$\frac{1}{2}$ teaspoon minced garlic
$1\frac{1}{2}$ cups mayonnaise collee (see Appendix)

2 tablespoons anchovy paste
1 teaspoon tomato paste
$\frac{1}{2}$ cup light cream
4 radishes, thinly sliced
2 teaspoons minced parsley
lemon slices

Remove yolks from the eggs and force through a sieve into a bowl. Beat in the butter, chives, salt, and pepper. Fill whites.

Sprinkle the cut side of the tomatoes with salt, pepper, sugar, and garlic. Place an egg, cut side down, on top of each tomato.

In a bowl, combine the mayonnaise, anchovy paste, tomato paste, and just enough light cream to make the mixture flow. Coat the eggs and tomatoes. Chill until set. Arrange the tomatoes on a platter and garnish with radish slices, minced parsley, and lemon slices.

Can be prepared the day before.

Serves 6.

Oeufs Durs en Tapenade
(Hard-Cooked Eggs with Olive-Anchovy Sauce)

24 black olives, pitted
 8 anchovy fillets
½ cup olive oil
 2 ounces tuna fish
 3 tablespoons capers, drained

lemon juice to taste
cognac to taste
 6 hard-cooked eggs, halved
12 ¼-inch thick tomato slices

In a blender or processor, puree the olives, anchovies, olive oil, tuna, and capers. Correct seasoning with lemon juice and cognac. Arrange egg halves, cut side down, on tomato slices and coat with the sauce.

Sauce can be prepared 2 to 3 days before. Arrange shortly before serving. Serves 6.

Oeufs Farcis au Cognac (Stuffed Eggs with Cognac)

 6 hard-cooked eggs, halved
 6 black olives, minced
2½ tablespoons capers, minced
 2 tablespoons cognac
 4 teaspoons tuna fish
½ teaspoon Dijon mustard

black pepper to taste
olive oil to taste
36 whole capers
 3 peeled tomatoes, sliced
 2 cups cold, cooked green beans
¾ cup vinaigrette

Remove the egg yolks and force through a sieve. In a bowl, beat the yolks with the olives, minced capers, cognac, tuna, mustard, plenty of black pepper, and just enough olive oil to bind. Mound the mixture into the whites and decorate with 3 capers each.

Arrange tomato slices on a platter. Toss the green beans with enough vinaigrette to coat lightly and put in the center of the platter. Lightly coat the tomatoes with some of the vinaigrette and top with the eggs. Coat eggs with the remaining vinaigrette.

For the best flavor, this dish should be served at just below room temperature. You can prepare the eggs, sauce, and beans the day before, but let them come to room temperature before arranging and serving.

Serves 6.

Above
Oeufs sur le Plat a la
Portugaise
Shirred Eggs Portuguese
(See page 59.)

Scallops Provencale with Spinach
Noodles
(See page 123.)

Above
Souffles aux
Crevettes a l'Estragon
*Shrimp Souffle with
Tarragon*
(See page 93.)

Huevos Fritos a
la Espagnola
Spanish Fried Eggs
(See page 67.)

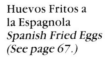

Sausages and Apples
(See page 139.)

Oeufs Durs Mistral
Hard-Cooked Eggs Mistral
(See page 52.)

Chicken Livers and Grapes
(See page 133.)

Gateau de Crepes aux Abricots
Cake of Crepes and Apricots
(See page 114.)

Oeufs Farcis au Cognac
Stuffed Eggs with Cognac
(See page 54.)

Oeufs sur le Plat au Fromage
Shirred Eggs with Cheese
(See page 57.)

Above
Zucchini and Ham Quiche
(See page 103.)

Oeufs sur le Plat Lully
Shirred Eggs Lully
(See page 61.)

Shirred Eggs Deerfoot
(See page 61.)

Oeufs Offenbach
*Scrambled Eggs with
Shrimp*
(See page 73.)

Above
Eggs Massena
(See page 38.)

Oeufs Brouilles Nicoise
Scrambled Eggs Nicoise
(See page 69.)

Above
Oeufs sur le Plat
Flamenco
Shirred Eggs Flamenco
(See page 61.)

Popovers with Scrambled
Eggs
(See page 70.)

Clam Pie
(See page 120.)

Oeufs Durs aux Crevettes (Hard-Cooked Eggs with Shrimp)

6 hard-cooked eggs, halved
1 pound shrimp, cooked, peeled,
   and deveined
¾ cup heavy cream, whipped

¾ cup mayonnaise
salt and pepper to taste
minced chives or dill

Place the eggs, round side up, in a serving dish and garnish with shrimp. Fold the cream into the mayonnaise and correct seasoning with salt and pepper. Coat the eggs with the sauce and sprinkle the chives over all.

Can be prepared the night before and refrigerated, covered.

Serves 6.

Oeufs Farcis a la Printaniere
(Stuffed Eggs with Vegetable and Rice Salad)

1 cup cold cooked rice
½ cup cooked diced carrots
½ cup cooked diced green beans
½ cup diced seeded cucumber
½ cup peeled, seeded, and diced
   tomato
½ cup tarragon vinaigrette

6 hard-cooked eggs, halved
8 tablespoons butter
4 ounces liver pate
4 ounces cream cheese
2 teaspoons tomato paste
bunch of watercress

In a 1½-quart bowl, toss the rice, carrots, beans, cucumber, and tomato pulp with the vinaigrette.

Remove the egg yolks, reserving whites, and force through a sieve. In a bowl, beat the egg yolks and butter to form a smooth paste. Transfer half of the mixture to another bowl and work in the liver pate. In the first bowl, beat in the cream cheese and tomato paste. Fill half of the egg whites with the liver mixture and the other half with the cheese-tomato mixture.

Arrange the rice salad on a serving platter and surround with the eggs. Garnish with watercress.

Can be prepared and stored covered in the refrigerator overnight. Should be served at or just below room temperature.

Serves 6.

✳ SHIRRED EGGS

In the past, shirred eggs (*oeufs sur le plat*) were a very popular egg preparation, but over the years their popularity has declined. Very possibly this is a result of stove design. When restaurants and homes had stoves with a large flat expanse of top, the egg dishes were safe. After stoves were designed with individual burners, porcelain dishes could not withstand the direct heat. It is possible, however, to make shirred eggs using the oven.

Shirred eggs are a delectable change from ordinary preparations and can be garnished attractively. Also, you can prepare a number of servings at one time, so you are not stranded in the kitchen cooking each serving separately. In flavor, a shirred egg is halfway between a fried egg and a poached egg.

Although many of these recipes call for individual dishes, you can prepare them in a large baking dish, if desired. Certainly, most households no longer have a dozen or more shirred egg dishes on hand. If you do, use them. If not, use a large shallow baking dish and prepare several servings at one time.

In the past, the filled dish was placed on the flat stove top to heat the bottom before being finished in the oven. Since this is impractical today (unless you have a griddle), put the dish in the oven to heat, preferably with enough butter just to film the bottom, before adding the eggs and remaining ingredients. Bake the eggs until the white is fully set and the yolk is still runny. For guests who do not like a runny yolk, bake the eggs longer.

Shirred eggs cannot be prepared ahead, but many of the garnishes can. If you have everything ready, the actual cooking time is brief. The time varies, depending on the temperature of the eggs and the accompanying food in the dish. Generally, they take 12 to 20 minutes to bake.

It is highly recommended that you break the eggs into a cup or saucer and slide them into the dish. Then if the yolk should break you can set that egg aside for another use.

Oeufs sur le Plat Omar Pacha (Shirred Eggs Omar Pascha)

12 tablespoons minced onions	12 tablespoons grated Parmesan
3 tablespoons butter	cheese
12 eggs	

Preheat oven to 350° F.

In a small skillet, saute the onions in the butter until very soft, but not browned. Meanwhile, heat egg dishes in the oven. Distribute the onions in the egg dishes and top with eggs. Sprinkle each egg with cheese and bake until set, about 10 minutes. Serve immediately.

Serves 6.

Oeufs sur le Plat au Fromage (Shirred Eggs with Cheese)

[handwritten: Simple & Good]

6 4-inch toast rounds *or other shape*	6 eggs
¼ cup melted butter	salt and pepper to taste
6 slices Gruyere cheese *or other*	6 tablespoons grated Gruyere cheese *or other*

Preheat oven to 350° F.

Dip the toast rounds in butter, arrange in 6 baking dishes, and top with a slice of cheese. Bake until the cheese melts. Place an egg on top of each slice of cheese and season with salt and pepper. Sprinkle with grated cheese and bake until set, about 10 minutes.

Serves 6.

Oeufs sur le Plat aux Haricots de Lima (Shirred Eggs with Lima Beans)

1 onion, thinly sliced	salt and pepper to taste
2 tablespoons butter	8 eggs
10 ounces cooked lima beans	3 tablespoons heavy cream
1 teaspoon minced parsley	2 tablespoons grated Parmesan cheese
1 tomato, peeled, ¼-inch dice	

Preheat oven to 350° F.

In a small skillet, saute the onion in the butter until tender. Stir in the beans, parsley, and tomato and correct seasoning with salt and pepper. Heat until hot. Divide among 4 heated egg dishes and add 2 eggs to each. Spoon the cream over the yolks and sprinkle with cheese. Bake until set.

Serves 4.

Oeufs sur le Plat a la Catalane (Shirred Eggs Catalonian)

6 thin slices eggplant	salt and pepper to taste
6 slices tomato	12 eggs
12 tablespoons butter	minced parsley
1 garlic clove, crushed	

Preheat oven to 350° F.

In a large skillet, saute the eggplant in half of the butter until tender. Remove and put each slice in a heated egg dish. Saute the tomatoes until tender in remaining butter. Drain and place on top of eggplant slices. Heat the garlic in butter remaining in the skillet until soft, but not browned. Season eggplant and tomato with salt and pepper and add 2 eggs to each dish. Season with salt and pepper and sprinkle eggs with garlic butter. Bake until set. Sprinkle with parsley.

Serves 6.

Oeufs sur le Plat a la Grecque (Shirred Eggs Grecian)

4 mushrooms, thinly sliced	2 onions, diced
6 tablespoons butter	1 green pepper, diced
½ teaspoon lemon juice	1 red pepper, diced
1 small eggplant, diced	2 tomatoes, peeled, seeded, and
2 tablespoons olive oil	chopped
1 orange cut in julienne	salt and pepper to taste
½ teaspoon crushed garlic	12 eggs
1 baking potato, boiled 3 minutes and diced	

Preheat oven to 350° F.

In a large skillet, saute the mushrooms in 3 tablespoons butter and lemon juice until tender. Remove from skillet and set aside.

In the same skillet, brown the eggplant in the olive oil. Remove and set aside.

Saute the orange rind and garlic in the remaining butter over low heat for 2 minutes, then add the potato and cook 3 minutes longer.

Add the onions and simmer for 2 minutes, then add the peppers and cook for 2 minutes more. Add the eggplant, mushrooms, and tomatoes to the skillet. Cook, stirring, for 5 minutes, or until all of the ingredients are tender. Correct seasoning with salt and pepper.

Divide mixture among 6 heated shirred egg dishes and add 2 eggs to each dish. Bake until set.

Serves 6.

Note: The success of this dish depends on how finely the vegetables have been diced. They should be no larger than half an inch.

Oeufs sur le Plat aux Champignons, Dit a la Polonaise (Shirred Eggs with Mushrooms)

¾ pound sliced mushrooms	1½ teaspoons lemon juice
4 tablespoons butter	12 large eggs
1½ cups Bechamel sauce	salt and pepper to taste
1 cup light cream	

Preheat oven to 350° F.

In a skillet, saute the mushrooms in the butter until tender. Stir in the Bechamel and light cream. Simmer for 10 minutes. Stir in lemon juice.

Divide the sauce among 6 heated shirred egg dishes. Make indentations in the sauce and slide the eggs into them. Season with salt and pepper. Bake until set.

Serves 6.

Oeufs sur le Plat a la Portugaise (Shirred Eggs Portuguese)

1½ cups tomato fondue (see Appendix)	salt and pepper to taste
	minced parsley
12 eggs	

Preheat oven to 350° F.

Place 1 tablespoon of tomato fondue in each of 6 egg dishes. Heat in the oven until hot. Add 2 eggs to each dish and season with salt and pepper. Bake until set.

Surround each egg with hot tomato fondue and sprinkle with minced parsley.

Serves 6.

Oeufs sur le Plat Lyonnaise (Shirred Eggs Lyonnaise)

2 cups minced onions
4 tablespoons butter

12 eggs
3 cups Lyonnaise sauce

Preheat oven to 350° F.

In a skillet, saute the onions in the butter until very soft and golden. Divide among 6 heated egg dishes and top each with 2 eggs. Surround the eggs with the sauce and bake until set.

Serves 6.

Shirred Eggs Borrachos

1½ cups hot lima bean puree (see
   Appendix)
12 slices cooked bacon
12 eggs

6 tablespoons butter
4 tablespoons dry red wine
salt and pepper to taste

Preheat oven to 350° F.

Divide the puree among 6 heated egg dishes. Top each with 2 slices of bacon and 2 eggs. In a saucepan, melt the butter and add the wine. Pour over the eggs. Season with salt and pepper. Bake until set.

Serves 6.

Oeufs sur le Plat a la Mexicaine (Shirred Eggs Mexican)

12 thin slices bacon, diced
12 slices tomato

6 canned chilies, minced
12 eggs

Preheat oven to 350° F.

Using 6 egg dishes, cook the bacon in the oven until crisp. Pour off excess fat. Add 2 tomato slices to each dish and top with 1 tablespoon of minced chili. Add the eggs to the dishes and bake until set.

Serves 6.

Oeufs sur le Plat Lully (Shirred Eggs Lully)

6 tablespoons butter
12 eggs
12 3-inch toast rounds
12 3-inch ham rounds
2 tablespoons butter
2 cups tomatoes, peeled, seeded,
   and chopped

3 tablespoons butter
¼ pound very fine egg noodles,
   cooked
salt and pepper to taste

Preheat oven to 350° F.

In each of 6 egg dishes, melt half a tablespoon of butter. Add 2 eggs to each dish and bake until set. Arrange 2 toast rounds on each serving plate. Saute the ham slices in 2 tablespoons butter until heated and place on top of toast. When eggs are set, arrange on top of ham. Meanwhile, saute the tomatoes in the remaining butter until hot. Fold into the noodles and season with salt and pepper. Arrange around the eggs.

Serves 6.

Shirred Eggs Deerfoot

12 breakfast sausages, half cooked
   and sliced
2 teaspoons butter

2 cups tomato sauce
2 teaspoons minced parsley
12 eggs

Preheat oven to 350° F.

In a saucepan, combine the sausages, butter, and tomato sauce. Simmer for 10 minutes. Add the parsley. Divide among 6 heated egg dishes and top with 2 eggs each. Bake until set.

Serves 6.

Oeufs sur le Plat Flamenco (Shirred Eggs Flamenco)

2 boiled potatoes, ½-inch cubes
4 chorizo sausages, ¼-inch slices
6 tablespoons butter
3 tomatoes peeled, seeded, ½-inch
   dice
3 canned pimientos, diced

4 tablespoons cooked peas
salt and pepper to taste
2 teaspoons minced parsley
12 eggs
4 tablespoons heavy cream
cayenne pepper to taste

Preheat oven to 350° F.

In a skillet, saute the potatoes and sausage in the butter until browned. Add the tomatoes, pimientos, peas, and salt and pepper to taste. Stir in the parsley and mix well. Divide among 6 heated egg dishes and top with 2 eggs each. Season eggs with salt and pepper. Bake 7 to 8 minutes. Spoon the cream over the eggs and bake until set. Sprinkle with cayenne.

Serves 6.

Oeufs en Surprise (Eggs in Tomato Cases)

6 medium tomatoes
salt and pepper to taste
2 tablespoons minced onion
2 tablespoons minced parsley
6 eggs

½ cup bread crumbs
2 tablespoons grated Parmesan cheese
2 tablespoons olive oil

Preheat oven to 350° F.

Remove the tops from the tomatoes and scoop out the centers. Drain. Season with salt and pepper and place tomatoes in a buttered casserole. Place a teaspoon of onion and parsley into each tomato and break an egg into each. Sprinkle the top with crumbs and cheese and drizzle with oil. Bake until set.

Serves 6.

Corned Beef Hash with Eggs

½ cup minced onions
2 tablespoons butter
1½ cups diced, cooked corned beef
2 cups diced, boiled potatoes

⅓ cup medium cream
salt and pepper to taste
6 eggs

Preheat oven to 350° F.

In a medium skillet, saute the onions in the butter until soft. Add the corned beef and potatoes and mix well. Stir in the cream, salt, and pepper and shape the mixture into 6 3-inch round patties, about 1 inch thick. Arrange the patties in buttered baking dishes and make an indentation in the center of each. Slide an egg into the center and season with salt and pepper. Bake until set.

Serves 6.

BAKED EGGS

In addition to shirred eggs, there are egg dishes that are baked in a water bath that provides gentle, even heat. You must have individual ramekins (they look like small souffle dishes) or custard cups to prepare these. Each one should hold ½ to ¾ of a cup. Very often, these eggs are served directly from the cup, but in some instances they are unmolded.

Water Bath

To make a water bath (bain marie), choose a baking pan large enough to hold the ramekins with about 1 inch of space between each one. Place the filled ramekins in the pan and add boiling water halfway up the sides.

Most often these recipes can be prepared for baking several hours ahead. Once baked, however, they should be served within minutes. They require 20 to 30 minutes to bake.

For guests who like to eat quiche without the crust, use the same ingredients, put them into ramekins or a souffle dish, and bake in a water bath.

Gebakken Eiren met Vien en Kaas *(Baked Eggs with Wine and Cheese)*

½ cup heavy cream
4 tablespoons grated Gruyere cheese
2 tablespoons lemon juice
2 tablespoons dry white wine

Dijon or Dusseldorf mustard to taste
salt and pepper to taste
8 eggs
buttered bread crumbs

Preheat oven to 350° F.

Butter 4 ramekins or custard cups. In a bowl, combine the cream, cheese, lemon juice, wine, mustard, salt, and pepper. Break 2 eggs into each ramekin and coat with cheese-wine mixture. Sprinkle with bread crumbs. Place in a water bath and bake until set.

Serves 4.

Oeufs Brayen (Baked Eggs Brayen)

6 eggs
6 tablespoons heavy cream
salt and pepper to taste

6 slices buttered toast
1 cup Bechamel sauce
minced parsley

Preheat oven to 350° F.

In a ½-quart bowl, beat the eggs, cream, salt, and pepper until well combined. Butter 6 ramekins. Pour the egg mixture into the ramekins and bake in a water bath until set, about 20 minutes. Unmold onto the toast slices, coat with Bechamel, and sprinkle with parsley.

Serves 6.

Oeufs en Cocotte (Baked Eggs with Celery Puree)

1 cup celery puree (see Appendix)	salt and pepper to taste
½ cup cream sauce	3 tablespoons heavy cream
6 eggs	minced fresh chervil

Preheat oven to 350° F.

In a bowl, combine the celery puree and cream sauce and divide among 6 ramekins or custard cups. Break an egg into each cup and season with salt and pepper to taste. Place in a water bath and bake until set. Before serving, coat the top of each egg with cream and sprinkle with chervil.

Serves 6.

Oeufs en Cocotte Lorraine (Baked Eggs Lorraine)

6 teaspoons minced, crisp bacon	12 eggs
18 thin slices Gruyere cheese	salt and pepper to taste
6 tablespoons boiling cream	

Preheat oven to 350° F.

Place a teaspoon of bacon in each ramekin and cover with 3 slices of Gruyere. Spoon 1 tablespoon of cream into each cup and break in 2 eggs. Season with salt and pepper and place cups in a water bath. Bake until set.

Serves 6.

Spanish Eggs

2 cups unsalted beef stock
2 cups minced ham
1 cup minced lean pork
½ cup minced onion
¼ cup butter
¼ cup flour

3 large tomatoes, peeled,
    seeded, and chopped
salt and pepper to taste
6 eggs
minced parsley

Preheat oven to 350° F.

In a saucepan, reduce the beef stock to 1 cup. In a medium skillet, saute the ham, pork, and onion in the butter until lightly browned.

In a small bowl, combine enough beef stock with the flour to make a slurry the consistency of heavy cream. Stir into the ham mixture with the remaining stock and tomatoes. Correct seasoning with salt and pepper. Simmer until thickened. Divide among 6 ramekins and add an egg to each. Place ramekins in a water bath and bake until set.

Serves 6.

Rigodon de Basse Bourgogne (Ham and Pork Custard)

½ pound sliced ham
½ pound cooked, sliced pork
3 cups milk
salt and pepper to taste

6 eggs, lightly beaten
⅓ cup flour
1 tablespoon butter

Preheat oven to 350° F.

Butter a 2-quart souffle dish well. Arrange the meats in alternating layers in the bottom. In a saucepan, bring the milk to a boil and season with salt and pepper. In a 2-quart bowl, beat the eggs with the flour and beat in the hot milk. Pour the custard over the meats and dot the top with butter. Place in a water bath and bake until set, about 40 minutes. Serve in wedges from the casserole dish. Can be served cold.

Serves 6.

Note: Be generous with the pepper. Also note, an Italian version of this recipe can be made using ¼ pound each of thinly sliced mortadella, Genoa salami, cappicola, and provolone.

FRIED EGGS

Although fried eggs with bacon, ham, or sausage is probably the quintessential American breakfast, there are few recipes in the literature for garnishing fried eggs beyond this. Perhaps the eggs are best appreciated on their own, or perhaps much of the literature comes from Europe, where other egg preparations are more popular. In France, the method of frying the egg is, in effect, deep frying. This sounds strange, and if you attempt it you may indeed wonder at the result. It is a time-consuming method and this author has never been able to prepare more than one egg at a time, which limits the number of guests you can serve. However, that can be true of properly prepared fried eggs in general.

To Fry Eggs

Use a small skillet, such as a 7-inch omelet pan. Melt 1 tablespoon of butter in the pan. Break the egg into a saucer as you would for poached eggs, and set aside any egg with a broken yolk for other uses. Slide the egg into the hot butter and let it cook over medium heat until the white is set.. During the cooking, spoon some of the hot butter over the yolk to cook the top. Keep the heat at medium. You may place a cover on the pan to help cook the yolk. When cooked, slip the egg onto a serving plate. A perfectly fried egg has a set, not a tough, white with no browned edges and a runny yolk.

To Fry Eggs French-Style

In an omelet pan, place about 4 tablespoons of vegetable oil. Heat until very hot but not smoking. Break an egg into a saucer. Have a dry wooden spoon at hand. Slide the egg into the oil and immediately tilt the pan by the handle to about a 45 degree angle so the oil and egg slide to one side. With a wooden spoon keep turning the egg in the oil to shape it into an oval. Cook, turning often, until the outside of the egg is golden. Drain on paper towels.

Oeufs a l'Espagnole (Fried Eggs Spanish-Style)

2 eggs, fried	4 tablespoons tomato sauce
2 tomato halves, sauteed in oil	1 teaspoon minced pimiento
½ cup fried onion rings	

In the center of a plate, arrange the eggs on top of the tomatoes, or adjacent to them. Fill the center of the plate between the yolks with the onion rings. In a saucepan, heat the tomato sauce and pimiento and coat each egg with the sauce, or place the sauce around the edge of the plate. The dish must be served as soon as prepared to be hot.

Serves 1.

Note: This recipe could be served with eggs fried French-style.

Huevos Fritos a la Espagnola (Spanish Fried Eggs)

This recipe is the Spanish, as opposed to the French, version of how the Spanish prepare fried eggs.

3 green peppers, chopped	salt and pepper to taste
1 large onion, chopped	4 fried eggs
4 tablespoons olive oil	8 toast points
4 tomatoes, peeled, seeded, and chopped	

In a 9-inch skillet, saute the peppers and onions in the oil until softened. Add tomatoes and cook until softened. Correct seasoning with salt and pepper. Simmer until thickened.

Place the vegetable mixture in the center of a platter, top with fried eggs, and garnish with toast points.

The sauce can be made the day before.

Serves 2 to 4.

Uova alla Salsa di Gambero (Eggs with Shrimp Sauce)

2 tablespoons minced onion	salt and pepper to taste
2 tablespoons minced parsley	6 tablespoons boiling water
2 tablespoons butter	12 shrimp, in shells
6 ounces shrimp, peeled and deveined	1 tablespoon butter
½ ounce toasted, ground pine nuts	6 fried eggs

In a 1-quart saucepan, saute the onion and parsley in the butter until tender. Add the shelled shrimp and pine nuts. Correct seasoning with salt and pepper and simmer until the shrimp are just cooked. Puree in a processor or blender with the water. In a small saucepan, reheat the sauce.

In a small skillet, saute the remaining shrimp until just cooked. Arrange the eggs on serving plates and surround with the sauce. Garnish with sauteed shrimp.

Serves 3 to 6.

Note: Traditionally, the shrimp are served in the shells. You may, of course, peel and devein them before sauteing. The shrimp can be of any size, but if they are small you may want to serve more than 2 to 4 per person.

Salisbury Steak with Fried Eggs

1 tablespoon minced green pepper	1 egg
1 tablespoon butter	salt, pepper, nutmeg, and thyme
1 pound lean ground beef	to taste
1 tablespoon minced parsley	6 slices toast
1 tablespoon minced onion	6 fried eggs
3 tablespoons bread crumbs	1½ cups tomato sauce

Preheat broiler.

Saute the pepper in the butter until soft. In a bowl, combine the pepper, beef, parsley, onion, bread crumbs, egg, salt, pepper, nutmeg, and thyme. Shape into 6 patties. Broil until medium rare. Place the patties on the toast, top with an egg, and surround with tomato sauce.

Serves 6.

Note: The beef patties are best cooked over a charcoal fire.

SCRAMBLED EGGS

The simplest of foods are often the most difficult to prepare. A perfectly roasted chicken or sauteed trout is more difficult to achieve than some of the more elaborate preparations. This maxim applies to scrambled eggs. They appear deceptively simple, but in fact are more difficult to produce perfectly than an omelet.

Scrambled eggs are made from eggs and seasoning. Creamy scrambled eggs are the result of careful, gentle cooking, not the addition of such liquids as milk, water, or cream. At the end of the cooking time, they should have a generous addition of butter, but only once they have set. To prepare them perfectly takes time, patience, and care. If you are in a hurry, make an omelet; if you have half an hour to spare, make scrambled eggs.

Scrambled eggs are perhaps at their best served only with buttered toast points. However, there are many accompaniments for them. Some of these recipes require the addition of other foods during the scrambling process, but it is still important to scramble the eggs gently over low heat.

You may have guests who prefer anything to a "loose" scrambled egg. In that case, you have no choice except to cook theirs longer. But even then, keep the heat low and cook them gently. High heat causes eggs to toughen and water to ooze from them.

Scrambled Eggs

12 eggs	8 tablespoons of butter
salt and pepper to taste	

In a 2-quart bowl, beat the eggs with salt and pepper until well mixed. For a creamier finish, strain the eggs through a sieve. This removes the chalaza, the tough white "thread" that holds the yolk in suspension in the white.

In a 9-inch skillet, melt 4 tablespoons of butter over low heat. Add the eggs and cook, stirring constantly, over low heat until the eggs are creamy and cooked, but not hard. Depending on how low the heat is, it will take 20 to 30 minutes for the eggs to cook. When almost cooked, stir in the remaining 4 tablespoons of butter. Once cooked, the eggs must be served immediately. Otherwise, they retain enough heat to continue to cook, so if you try to hold them they will lose some of their creaminess.

Serves 4 to 6.

Note: For large crowds, it is possible to prepare the eggs in a double boiler. Use a standard double boiler or, if necessary, construct one by inserting one kettle into another. The water in the bottom should never boil. As soon as the eggs are warm to the touch, keep stirring from the bottom for even cooking.

Oeufs Brouilles Nicoise (Scrambled Eggs Nicoise)

1 cup cubed slab bacon	1 tablespoon minced parsley
2 cups warm eggplant provencale	1 teaspoon lemon juice
(see Appendix)	12 eggs, scrambled
4 tablespoons unsalted butter	4 tablespoons butter

In a 9-inch skillet, cook the bacon in its own fat until almost crisp. Drain off excess fat. Add the eggplant mixture to the skillet and heat.

In a bowl, beat the butter with the parsley and lemon juice until combined. Scramble eggs in butter. When the eggs are almost set, stir in the parsley butter. Arrange eggs on a serving platter and surround with eggplant mixture. Serve at once.

Serves 4 to 6.

Scrambled Eggs in Tomato Cups

6 medium tomatoes	12 eggs, scrambled
salt and pepper	12 anchovy fillets, drained

Preheat oven to 350° F.

Cut off top third of the tomatoes. Hollow out and season with salt and pepper. Place in a baking dish and heat in the oven. Scramble eggs according to directions. Place a tomato cup on a serving plate, fill with eggs, and arrange 2 anchovy fillets over the top. Serve at once.

Serves 6.

Oeufs Brouilles a l'Alice (Scrambled Eggs Alice)

6 large cream puffs (see Appendix)	salt and pepper to taste
6 mushroom caps	12 eggs, scrambled
1 tablespoon butter	6 slices crisp, warm bacon

Preheat oven to 350° F.

Warm the cream puffs in the oven. In a skillet, saute the mushroom caps in the butter until tender. Season with salt and pepper. With a sharp knife, cut off the top third of the cream puffs. Fill with scrambled eggs and garnish with bacon and sauteed mushrooms. Serve immediately.

Serves 6.

Popovers with Scrambled Eggs

6 popovers (see index for recipe)	12 eggs, scrambled
	2 tablespoons minced chives

Preheat oven to 350° F.

Place popovers in the oven to heat. Scramble eggs according to directions. At the end, stir in the chives. Cut open the popovers and fill with eggs. Serve immediately.

Serves 6.

Sausage Cups with Chive Scrambled Eggs

1½ pounds mild sausage meat
  1 tablespoon minced onion
  1 cup uncooked rolled oats
  1 egg

¼ cup milk
12 eggs, scrambled
 6 ounces cream cheese with
   chives, in ½-inch cubes

Preheat oven to 325° F.

In a bowl, combine the sausage, onion, oats, egg, and milk. Press the mixture into 6 muffin tins or custard cups, forming a hollow center in each. Bake for 30 minutes.

Drain off excess fat and place sausage cups on paper towels. Keep warm.

Scramble the eggs according to directions and, when almost cooked, stir in the cheese. The cheese does not have to melt completely, but it should be warm. Serve in sausage cups.

Serves 6.

Scrambled Eggs with Snail Toasts

 8 tablespoons butter
 1 clove garlic, crushed
 1 teaspoon minced parsley
⅛ teaspoon lemon juice
24 toast fingers

24 snails, drained and rinsed
¼ cup shredded Gruyere
  cheese
12 eggs, scrambled with
  chives

Preheat oven to 425° F.

In a bowl, cream the butter until light and fluffy. Beat in the garlic, parsley, and lemon juice. Spread the toasts with half of the butter, top with snails, and dot with remaining butter. Sprinkle with cheese. Place on a baking sheet. Heat in the oven for 3 to 5 minutes, or until cheese is melted. Arrange scrambled eggs on serving plate and surround with snail toasts. Serve immediately.

Serves 6.

Uova alla Milano (Eggs Milan)

3 tablespoons butter	1 cup dry white wine
1/4 pound grated Parmesan cheese	8 eggs, beaten
1 tablespoon minced shallots	salt, pepper, and nutmeg to taste
1 tablespoon minced chives	16 toast triangles

In a 9-inch skillet, melt the butter and stir in the cheese, shallots, and chives. Cook, stirring, over low heat gradually stirring in the wine until the mixture is smooth. Pour in the eggs and cook, stirring, over very low heat. These will be extremely loose. Correct seasoning. Serve on a warm platter and garnish with toast triangles. Serve immediately.

Serves 4.

Scrambled Eggs with Smoked Salmon

1/2 cup minced onions	12 eggs, scrambled
4 tablespoons butter	black pepper to taste
1 pound thinly sliced smoked salmon	minced parsley to taste

In a 7-inch skillet, saute the onions in the butter until soft, but not brown. Stir in the smoked salmon and just heat through. Stir the onion and salmon mixture into the eggs just before they are set. Arrange eggs on serving plates and sprinkle generously with pepper and parsley. Serve immediately.

Serves 4 to 6.

Lox and Eggs

1 large onion, minced	1 tablespoon minced parsley
1 green pepper, minced	
2 cups sliced mushrooms	1/4 teaspoon minced fresh basil
8 tablespoons butter	
1/2 pound lox, chopped	Tabasco sauce to taste
8 eggs	salt and pepper to taste

In a 10-inch skillet, saute the onion, pepper, and mushrooms in the butter until soft. Lower the heat. Add the salmon and cook until just heated.

In a 2-quart bowl, beat the eggs, parsley, basil, Tabasco, salt, and pepper until well mixed. Add to the salmon mixture and scramble over low heat until just set. Serve immediately.

Serves 4.

Note: Add salt sparingly, depending on the saltiness of the smoked salmon.

Oeufs Offenbach (Scrambled Eggs with Shrimp)

2 large tomatoes, peeled and seeded	3 ounces tuna fish, flaked
2 tablespoons butter	6 slices buttered toast
12 eggs, scrambled	12 medium shrimp, cooked and peeled
3 anchovy fillets, minced	2 tablespoons minced parsley

Cut tomatoes into 6 1/4-inch slices. Dice remainder. In a 9-inch skillet, saute the tomato slices in the butter until heated through.

When eggs are almost set, stir in the anchovies and tuna fish. Place toast on hot plates and put a tomato slice on top. Spoon eggs over tomatoes and garnish with the shrimp, diced tomatoes, and parsley.

Serves 6.

Scrambled Eggs a la Caracas

2 ounces smoked dried beef, minced	1/4 cup minced onion
3 cups peeled, seeded, and chopped tomatoes	pinch of cinnamon
	pinch of cayenne
3/4 cup grated Parmesan cheese	6 tablespoons butter
	9 eggs, beaten

In a 10-inch skillet, saute the beef, tomatoes, cheese, onion, cinnamon, and cayenne in the butter until tomatoes are soft and the liquid has evaporated. Stir in eggs and scramble until set. Serve immediately.

Serves 4 to 6.

OMELETS

Omelet making is one of those areas of cooking surrounded by mystique and legend, which in fact have little to do with the production of fine omelets.

Some people happily announce that they have never washed their omelet pan—all too often you know it! If you make omelets often, at least once a week, then wiping the pan with paper toweling and salt is an acceptable practice. However, if you make omelets less than once a month, an unwashed pan can be unpleasant, if not unhealthy. The oil retained in the pan can turn rancid.

Omelet Pans

An omelet pan (sauteuse) has a flat bottom with gently sloping sides. Traditionally, it is made of steel, which transfers heat immediately to the contents of the pan. These pans rust easily and they are prone to sticking unless well seasoned. The alacrity with which they allow you to make omelets may not compensate for their maintenance problems.

Aluminum omelet pans are used in most professional kitchens in the United States. They can be polished to a mirror brightness with steel wool pads, and are easily seasoned and useful for cooking other foods. After a period of reasonable use, it is often possible to make omelets without re-seasoning the pan, unless you have had to scrape off some burned food.

There are many nonstick pans available that make omelet-making easy and cut maintenance to almost nothing. These have the advantage of being useful for foods other than omelets, a reasonable consideration if storage is a problem.

To Season an Omelet Pan

Scour the pan with steel wool pads, rinse well, and dry. Put about 1 inch of unflavored salad oil into the pan and place over very low heat until the oil is very hot, but not smoking (about one hour). Turn off the heat and cool the oil in the pan. Drain off the oil (you can use it for deep frying) and wipe the pan with paper toweling. This process may seem like too much work for one omelet, but if you are serving several, seasoning the pan a day or two before is worth the trouble.

To Cook an Omelet

A three-egg, single-serving omelet is the most reasonable size to make. It will cook quickly and easily. If you need omelets for more than one person, this size can be made quickly enough to serve everyone without delay. Larger omelets are difficult to make and take as long as several smaller ones.

Break the eggs into a bowl, season with salt and pepper, and beat about 40 vigorous strokes with a fork. Some cooks believe that 1 tablespoon of water for each 3-egg portion makes a lighter omelet. Over high heat, heat the pan until very hot. Add 1 tablespoon of butter, which should start to sizzle immediately, bubble up, and begin to smell nut-like. Pour in the eggs and let them set about 5 seconds. Hold a fork with the tines horizontal to the pan and stir the eggs in a circle while shaking the pan back and forth with the other hand. It's rather like trying to rub your stomach while patting your head. If you keep both hands close to one another it will be easier. The object is to keep the egg mixture moving so that it does not stick to the pan.

As the omelet begins to set, pull the sides toward the center and lift the edges to let the uncooked egg flow underneath. When the center of the omelet is almost set, but still moist, place the filling in a line across the center. Tilt the pan up and back toward the handle and use the sloping sides of the pan and a fork to help turn one third of the omelet over the filling. Put the pan on the side of the stove and place the palm of your hand under the handle with your thumb pointing away from the pan. Grasp the handle firmly. In one fluid movement tilt the pan in the opposite direction, to fold the omelet in thirds. Turn the omelet out onto a plate into a neat yellow oval. Perfectly cooked omelets are not browned because browning changes the flavor. If you have a guest who is convinced that no egg is cooked unless it is browned, cook the omelet a few minutes longer.

Serve omelets immediately while they are still light and puffy. The slightly undercooked center will continue to cook from the heat of the omelet and the filling. The whole process takes only 30 to 45 seconds.

Omelets for a Crowd

Omelets do not hold. They must be served immediately and therefore have to be made to order. It is possible to set up a production line to serve people quickly. You will probably want to practice before attempting to serve a number of guests. Entertaining can be difficult enough without starting your day cooking under intense pressure.

Allow 3 eggs for each omelet. Break all the eggs into a bowl, season with salt and pepper, and beat well. Strain the eggs to ensure that they are well beaten and that there are no bits of shell. Use a 6-ounce ladle to measure each omelet and follow the previous directions. With a little practice, you will be able to serve 6 people in less than 5 minutes.

If you are offering a selection of fillings, have your guests make their choices before you start to cook their omelet. No one wants to wait for some guest to decide while you have a cooked omelet in hand.

Folding and Filling Omelets

Omelets can be folded in several ways. The classic method is to put the filling in the center third and fold over the two sides as described. Sometimes the omelet is folded and turned out without any filling, a slit is cut along the length of the omelet, and the filling is put into the slit. On occasion the filling is put on half of the omelet and covered with the other half. Also, you can slide the unfolded omelet onto a plate and place the filling on top.

Fillings for omelets are limitless; you are not restricted to the few suggestions here. For example, many of the fillings for crepes, or the meat and fish preparations in other chapters, are suitable fillings for omelets. Remember that omelets began as the thrifty French housewife's answer to stretching leftovers. If you want to serve lobster or caviar on a limited budget, using a small amount in an omelet is one way of appearing extravagant while watching your wallet.

Other Types of Omelets

In addition to the classic folded omelet, there are the flat, pancake-like frittata, found in areas around the Mediterranean, and the omelet souffle.

The frittata usually has chopped foods mixed in with the eggs. It is poured into a large, heated, well-buttered or oiled skillet, and cooked until set and browned on the bottom. It is then slid onto a large plate and flipped over into the pan to finish cooking the other side. Frittatas are served cut into wedges. They can be eaten at room temperature and are especially pleasant at a picnic.

Omelet souffles are similar to souffles in that they are made by separating the eggs and adding the flavoring to the yolks. The whites are beaten until stiff and folded into the yolks. The heated omelet pan is filled with the egg mixture and allowed to set for a few minutes on medium heat on top of the stove. The pan is then put into a 425° F. oven and baked until the omelet is puffed and cooked. It must be served immediately.

Omelette Fines Herbes (Omelet with Herbs)

3 eggs
salt and pepper to taste

1 tablespoon mixed, fresh minced parsley, chervil, chives, and tarragon
1 tablespoon butter

In a bowl, beat the eggs with the salt, pepper, and herbs about 40 vigorous strokes. In a hot omelet pan, melt the butter. Add the eggs and cook, shaking the pan back and forth and stirring with a fork until almost set. Tilt the omelet back toward the handle, reverse your hand and tilt out onto a serving plate. Serve at once.

Serves 1.

Princess Omelet

8 eggs	6 ounces cream cheese,
½ cup sour cream	¼-inch cubes
4 teaspoons minced onion	butter
pinch of cayenne pepper	1 pound cooked, hot
½ teaspoon salt	asparagus

In a bowl, combine the eggs, sour cream, onion, pepper, and salt. Stir in the cream cheese. In a hot omelet pan, heat the butter and use the mixture to make 4 omelets. Fill each omelet with a few spears of asparagus and use any remaining spears as a garnish.

Serves 4.

Note: You must work quickly. If the cream cheese melts and sticks to the pan you will have difficulty in turning out the omelet.

Omelette a l'Arlesienne
(Omelet with Eggplant and Tomatoes)

1 recipe eggplant provencale (see	2 3-egg omelets
Appendix)	minced parsley

Have the eggplant mixture prepared and hot. Make the omelets and fill with the eggplant mixture. Turn out and garnish with minced parsley.

Eggplant mixture can be made 2 to 3 days ahead and reheated.

Serves 2.

Omelette Savoyarde
(Folded Omelet with Potatoes and Cheese)

1 cup sliced boiled potatoes	salt and pepper to taste
4 tablespoons butter	2 3-egg omelets
⅓ cup shredded Gruyere cheese	minced parsley
¼ cup heavy cream	

In a 7-inch skillet, heat the potatoes in the butter. Stir in the cheese, cream, salt, and pepper. Keep warm. Prepare omelets. Fill with potato mixture and fold. Sprinkle with minced parsley.

Potato mixture can be made the day before and gently reheated.

Serves 2.

Omelette au Broccio (Omelet with Goat Cheese)

6 eggs
large pinch of minced fresh mint
salt and pepper to taste

3 tablespoons butter
1 cup Broccio, or other goat cheese
mint sprigs

In a bowl, beat the eggs with the fresh mint, salt, and pepper. Make 2 omelets. When almost set, crumble the cheese in the center and fold. Turn onto a heated platter and garnish with the mint sprigs.
Serves 2.

Omelette Gargamelle (Mushroom and Cheese Omelet)

2 cups minced mushrooms
3 scallions, minced
5 tablespoons dry vermouth
¾ cup heavy cream
salt and pepper to taste

1 teaspoon cornstarch
3 3-egg omelets
1 tablespoon grated Parmesan cheese
3 thin slices Gruyere cheese
paprika

Preheat broiler.
In a 1-quart saucepan, simmer the mushrooms, scallions, vermouth, and ½ cup heavy cream for 5 minutes. Correct seasoning. In a small bowl, combine the remaining cream and cornstarch and add to the pan. Cook stirring until thickened.
Prepare the omelets and fill, using only half of the creamed mixture. Arrange cooked omelets in ovenproof baking dishes and pour on the remaining cream mixture. Add cheeses and sprinkle with paprika. Broil until golden brown. Serve at once.
You cannot prepare these ahead for broiling. As soon as they are made, they should be glazed and served.
Serves 3.

Royal Omelet

2 ounces grated Parmesan cheese
1 ounce butter
1 cup heavy cream

6 eggs
3 tablespoons heavy cream
1 tablespoon grated Parmesan cheese

Preheat broiler.

In a saucepan, melt the 2 ounces of cheese in the butter over low heat and stir in the 1 cup of cream. Heat, stirring, until thickened. Do not boil. Set aside.

Prepare 2 omelets and turn into ovenproof baking dishes. Coat the omelets with the sauce and sprinkle with remaining cream and cheese. Glaze under the broiler. Serve immediately.

Serves 2.

Omelet with Ricotta and Salami

½ cup ricotta cheese
½ cup diced Genoa salami
salt and pepper to taste

3 3-egg omelets
butter, softened

In a small bowl, combine the ricotta and salami and season with salt and pepper. The ingredients must be at least at room temperature. If necessary, cover and place in a 350° F. oven for 10 minutes to warm them.

Prepare the omelets, fill with the ricotta mixture, and turn out. Brush the surface of the omelets with butter and cut a slit to expose the filling. Serve at once.

Serves 3.

Omelette a la Bourguignonne (Omelet with Snails)

⅓ cup minced onions
⅓ cup minced shallots
2 tablespoons minced garlic
2 tablespoons butter
4 tablespoons flour
1 cup whole stewed tomatoes,
   drained

4½-ounce can snails
¼ cup minced, cooked carrots
salt and pepper to taste
2 3-egg omelets

In a skillet, saute the onion, shallots, and garlic in butter until tender. Stir in the flour and cook over low heat until golden. Stir in the tomatoes and ¼ cup of liquid from snails. Cook, stirring, until thickened and smooth. Add the snails, carrots, and salt and pepper to taste. Simmer 10 to 15 minutes.

Prepare the omelets, fill with snail mixture, and fold. Serve immediately.

Serves 2.

L'Omelette Baron du Barante
(Lobster and Mushroom Omelet)

1½ pounds mushrooms, sliced	½ cup heavy cream
4 tablespoons butter	1 pound lobster meat, sliced
salt and pepper to taste	6 3-egg omelets
½ cup dry port	grated Parmesan cheese

In a 9-inch skillet, saute the mushrooms in the butter until the liquid has evaporated. Season lightly with salt and pepper. Stir in port and cream and reduce by half. Correct seasoning with salt and pepper. Add lobster and reheat gently. If you boil it, the lobster will be tough.

Prepare the omelets and fill with lobster mixture. Serve immediately. Serves 6.

Brazilian Omelet

½ pound lean ground beef	1 teaspoon chili powder
1-pound can stewed tomatoes	salt to taste
1 small green pepper, julienne	¼ teaspoon sugar
1 tablespoon minced green chilies	4 3-egg omelets

In a 9-inch skillet, brown the beef in its own fat. Drain off excess fat. Stir in tomatoes, pepper, chilies, chili powder, salt, and sugar. Simmer for 5 minutes.

Prepare the omelets and fill with the mixture. Slit the omelets lengthwise to expose the filling.
Serves 4.

Omelet Benedict

½ cup diced lean ham	2 3-egg omelets
½ teaspoon butter	1 cup tarragon-flavored Mousseline
½ cup tiny fried croutons	sauce (see Appendix)

Preheat broiler.

In a 7-inch skillet, saute the ham in the butter until hot. Add the croutons and heat. Prepare the omelets and fill with the ham mixture. Fold and coat the omelets with the sauce. Glaze until golden.
Serves 2.

Omelette aux Pissenlits (Omelet with Dandelion Greens)

1 bunch dandelion greens, washed
  and chopped
1/4-inch thick slice country ham, diced
1 tablespoon butter

9 eggs
salt and pepper to taste
pinch of ground coriander
3 tablespoons lard

In a 9-inch skillet, saute the greens and ham in the butter until heated through. Beat the eggs with the salt, pepper, and coriander. Stir in the greens and ham.

Using the lard, prepare 3 omelets, letting them brown lightly before folding and turning out. Serve at once.

Serves 3.

Omelette a la Bearnaise (Omelet Bearn-Style)

5 ounces pickled peppers, cornichons, or capers in vinegar
1/4 pound lean bacon, diced
2 tablespoons of oil

1 tablespoon tomato puree
9 eggs, lightly beaten
salt and pepper to taste
3 tablespoons butter

Drain the peppers, cornichons, or capers and mince. In a 7-inch skillet, saute the bacon in the oil until browned. Drain and discard fat. Stir in the peppers and tomato puree and simmer 1 minute. Let mixture cool for 1 minute then stir into the eggs. Correct seasoning with salt and pepper. Prepare 3 omelets, using the butter. Serve immediately.

Serves 3.

Note: Although *Bearnaise* in cooking generally refers to a sauce similar to Hollandaise, there is a region of France called the Bearn where this recipe originated.

Omelette Normande (Apple Omelet)

1 1/2 pounds apples, peeled, cored,
  and sliced
3 tablespoons butter

3 3-egg omelets
3 tablespoons Calvados
sugar

Preheat broiler.

In a 9-inch skillet, saute the apples in butter and 1 tablespoon Calvados until tender. Prepare omelets, fill with apples, fold, and turn onto a heat-proof platter. Sprinkle omelets with sugar and glaze until golden brown. Flame with the remaining Calvados. Serve immediately.

Serves 3 to 6.

Note: To flame the Calvados, warm it in a small saucepan over low heat. Pour over the omelet and ignite with a match. Make sure that it is not too close to you or your guests. You may substitute almost any fruit for the apples and will probably wish to change the liqueur as well. For example, Grand Marnier with oranges or strawberries, kirsch with strawberries or raspberries, and rum with peaches or grapes.

Sweet Omelet Souffle

8 eggs, separated	¼ teaspoon salt
1 cup sugar	2 tablespoons butter
flavoring (see note)	

Preheat oven to 425° F.

In a bowl, beat the egg yolks with ½ cup of sugar and the liquid flavoring of your choice until they are light in color, smooth, very thick, and form a ribbon.

In a separate bowl, beat the egg whites with the salt until they form soft peaks. Add the remaining sugar, 1 tablespoon at a time, beating the whites until they are stiff and glossy. Fold the egg whites into the egg yolks. Fold in other flavoring as listed in the note, if desired.

In a deep 10-inch skillet with a heatproof handle, melt the butter over medium heat. Spread ¾ of the batter in the skillet, smoothing the surface. Put the remaining batter into a pastry bag fitted with a #6 B tip and pipe rosettes and swirls over the souffle. Place the pan over medium heat and cook 3 minutes, or until the bottom is set. Transfer the pan to the oven and bake 8 minutes in the upper third of the oven until the top is puffed, firm, and golden brown. Serve at once.

Serves 6 to 8.

Note: For flavorings, use 1 tablespoon of vanilla, or 2 tablespoons of a favorite liqueur to flavor the egg yolks. If you wish, you can fold in ½ to ¾ cup of toasted ground almonds, walnuts, pecans, or hazelnuts. For texture and additional flavor, minced fresh fruit can also be folded in. Use about 1 cup of well-drained fruit.

Kaiserschmarrn

⅔ cup raisins
2 ounces cognac
4 tablespoons sugar
5 eggs, separated
1 cup heavy cream

1 cup flour
6 tablespoons butter
4 tablespoons sugar
confectioners' sugar

Preheat oven to 350° F.

Butter 2-quart souffle dish.

In a small bowl, macerate the raisins in the brandy for at least 30 minutes. Stir 4 tablespoons of sugar into the egg yolks and add the heavy cream, stirring constantly. Add the flour gradually, stirring constantly until the batter is smooth. Beat the egg whites until stiff but not dry. Fold into the batter. Pour into the souffle dish and bake for 10 to 15 minutes, or until the omelet is puffed and golden.

Melt 6 tablespoons of butter in a skillet. With a fork, tear the omelet into pieces about 1½ inches square. Put the pieces into a skillet with the cognac-raisin mixture and 4 tablespoons of sugar. Saute the chunks until they have a light coating of butter and sugar. Sprinkle with confectioners' sugar. Serve immediately.

Serves 4 to 6.

Note: This somewhat strange recipe is reputed to have been the favorite of Emperor Franz Joseph. It is in fact delicious and makes a very pleasant brunch dish.

Frittata di Zucchini (Italian Flat Zucchini Omelet)

2 small zucchini, thinly sliced
flour
3 tablespoons olive oil
6 eggs, lightly beaten

1 tablespoon grated Parmesan cheese
salt and pepper to taste
pinch of ground thyme

Dredge the zucchini in flour. Saute in olive oil in a 10-inch skillet until golden brown and tender.

In a bowl, combine the eggs, cheese, salt, pepper, and thyme. Pour over the zucchini in the skillet and cook until set and browned on one side. Slide onto a plate and flip over into the pan. Brown on the other side. Serve cut into wedges.

Serves 2 to 4.

Frittata di Porri (Leek Frittata)

5 large leeks, white part only,
   ½-inch thick slices
4 tablespoons olive oil

6 eggs
salt and pepper to taste

Place sliced leeks in a medium bowl and cover with cold water. Soak 20 minutes. Drain and rinse carefully under cold running water. Dry well. In a 10-inch skillet, heat 3 tablespoons olive oil. Add leeks and saute until softened. Transfer to a bowl and let cool. Beat eggs with salt and pepper to taste. Add sauteed leeks. In a 10-inch skillet, heat remaining tablespoon of oil until hot. Add egg mixture and cook as described for Frittata di Zucchini.

South American Omelet

1 large avocado, halved
8 eggs
salt and pepper to taste

1 tablespoon olive oil
2 tablespoons butter

Using a melon baller, make small balls of half of the avocado. Cut the remaining avocado into ½-inch cubes. Beat the eggs with the salt and pepper and add diced avocado. Cook in the oil and butter to make a flat omelet. Turn out and garnish with avocado balls.
   Serves 3 to 4.

Omelette Ropa Vieja (Cuban "Old Clothes" Omelet)

2 tomatoes, peeled, seeded, and
   chopped
2 tablespoons butter

½ cup shredded chicken or ham
4 eggs, lightly beaten
1 tablespoon minced parsley

Heat the tomatoes in the butter. Add the chicken or ham and cook until slightly thickened. Add the eggs and parsley and cook over low heat until set and lightly browned. Turn and brown the other side.
   Serves 1 to 2 persons.

Omelette aux Noix (Walnut Omelet)

8 eggs
salt and pepper to taste

20 walnuts
3 tablespoons butter

In a bowl, beat the eggs with salt and pepper to taste.

In a 10-inch skillet, heat the walnuts in the butter until the butter is foamy. Pour in the eggs and cook until lightly browned on one side. Remove from the pan, turn over, and return to the pan to brown the other side. Serves 3 to 4.

Omelette a la Savoyarde (Flat Savoy Omelet)

2 boiled potatoes, thinly sliced
7 tablespoons butter
8 eggs, lightly beaten

¼ cup grated Gruyere cheese
1 teaspoon chervil
salt and pepper to taste

In a 9-inch skillet, saute the potatoes in 6 tablespoons butter until browned.

In a medium bowl, combine the eggs, Gruyere, chervil, salt, and pepper. Mix well. Pour over the potatoes and mix potatoes so eggs settle to the bottom of the pan. Let cook undisturbed until golden. Run a flexible spatula under the omelet to loosen and slide out onto a plate. Add the remaining butter to the pan and return the omelet, the uncooked side down. Cook until browned.

Serves 3 to 4.

La Piperade du Pays Basque (Basque Pepper Omelet)

1 green pepper, thinly sliced
1 tablespoon olive oil
4 tomatoes, peeled, seeded, and
   chopped
1 onion, thinly sliced

½ clove garlic, crushed
¼ cup diced ham
salt and pepper to taste
2 tablespoons butter
4 eggs

In a 7-inch skillet, saute the pepper in the olive oil until soft. Add the tomatoes, onion, garlic, and ham and season with salt and pepper. Add the butter and simmer until tomatoes are a soft puree and the mixture is slightly thickened.

Beat the eggs and season with salt and pepper. Add to the vegetable mixture in the skillet and cook until barely set. Turn out and serve.

Serves 1 to 2.

Note: This particular version of a flat omelet is served barely set, not browned on both sides.

CHAPTER 4
Souffles

Souffles, like omelets, strike terror into the hearts of many otherwise justifiably confident cooks. In fact, they are simple and thrifty ways to use leftovers. A souffle is nothing more than a Bechamel (cream) sauce enriched with egg yolks, flavored with cheese, vegetables, fish, or meat, and leavened with beaten egg whites. Once the souffle has been assembled, it can be kept in the refrigerator for an hour or so before baking.

BASIC SOUFFLE MIXTURE

Bechamel Sauce

3 tablespoons butter	1½ cups milk
3 tablespoons flour	

In a 1-quart saucepan, melt the butter, stir in the flour, and cook the roux until it starts to turn golden. Stir in the milk and cook, stirring, until the mixture is thick and smooth. Simmer, stirring often, until reduced to 1 cup. The sauce will be thick.

Enough for a 1-quart souffle.

Note: There are recipes for souffles that do not use a Bechamel base, but rather have the egg yolks beaten into a heated puree.

Egg Yolks

The egg yolks, 4 for the amount of Bechamel given in the recipe, are beaten into the sauce one at a time over heat. Bring the mixture just to the boil to form the liaison between the sauce and the yolks. Now beat in the flavoring.

Puree Flavoring

The flavoring for a souffle can be pureed vegetables, such as cauliflower, corn, or spinach, but often the flavoring is more pronounced if it is treated differently. For example, use grated cheese or finely ground chicken or ham.

Sometimes the best flavor results from slicing the food, combining it with a cream sauce, and putting in the bottom of the dish. A cheese souffle is placed on top and the dish is baked in the usual manner. The flavor from the sauce mixture perfumes the cheese souffle and is used as a sauce when it is served.

After the flavoring has been added to the sauce, you can cover it and chill overnight, if desired. Reheat the sauce mixture before adding the egg whites.

Egg Whites

The egg whites, usually one or two more than the number of yolks, are beaten with a pinch of salt until stiff, but not dry. If you overbeat them, they will not hold up the souffle. Gently fold the whites into the flavored sauce. If the sauce mixture is very thick, stir in about one quarter of the beaten egg whites to loosen the sauce. Do not worry if they deflate. Then gently fold in the remaining whites, taking care that they do not deflate. At this point, you can refrigerate the souffle, covered, for an hour.

SOUFFLE DISHES

Although the customary souffle dish is white porcelain with a flat bottom and straight sides, you can use any flat-bottomed, straight-sided ovenproof container. The author has used saucepans, charlotte molds, and even cake tins. You can bake a souffle in a rectangular baking dish, but it will not be as impressive. Your chosen dish should be about one quart in size. It is possible to make larger souffles, but they usually do not rise as impressively or cook as evenly. If you need more than four servings, make two one-quart souffles or more, rather than one huge souffle.

Souffles can be made very successfully in individual souffle dishes, ramekins, or custard cups. Each guest gets an individual serving that holds up better because it does not have to be cut into serving portions. If you are making individual souffles, heat a baking sheet in the oven and place the souffles on it to bake. Then you can remove them all at once to serve.

Butter the inside of the dish generously and sprinkle it with fresh bread crumbs or sugar, depending on the type of souffle. If the souffle mixture is thick enough to mound, it is not necessary to collar the dish. Just run your thumb around the edge of the dish to separate the mixture from the dish. It will help you give a top hat to your souffle. If the mixture is too thin or you want a very tall souffle, attach a collar.

To Collar a Souffle Dish

Cut a piece of metal foil, parchment paper, or waxed paper long enough to encircle the souffle dish and overlap. Fold the collar in half lengthwise. It should extend as high above the rim of the dish as below it. Tie securely in place with string; if you are using foil, you can crimp it. Butter the upper inside half of the collar.

BAKING A SOUFFLE

Put the baking rack in the lowest position possible. If you have a gas stove, you can bake the souffle on the floor of the oven. Preheat the oven to 375° F. for an entree souffle or 425° F. for a dessert souffle. Bake an entree souffle for 25 to 35 minutes and a dessert souffle for 15 to 20 minutes. Serve immediately.

Although a souffle can be held before baking, once it is baked time is of the essence. If you try to hold the souffle, you will likely end up serving a sunken pancake.

WHEN IS A SOUFFLE COOKED?

Generally, in France, a souffle is done when the outside is golden brown and the center is very hot, but still somewhat fluid. The moisture in the center is expected to serve as a sauce for the outer edges of the souffle. Americans seem to prefer souffles that are cooked more fully and that have an almost cake-like consistency throughout. It is up to you as to how you serve the souffle.

ROLLED SOUFFLE

For a number of guests, it may be easier to make a rolled souffle rather than the traditional version. The souffle mixture is baked in a sponge roll pan and unmolded. Often a filling is laid along its edge and the mixture is rolled like a jelly roll and placed on a serving dish. A sauce may be served over the top. The texture of a rolled souffle is somewhat firmer than a regular souffle, which makes it easier to cut the souffle into slices. A rolled souffle will not hold up much longer than a regular souffle.

Souffle au Fromage (Cheese Souffle)

3 tablespoons butter	pinch of grated nutmeg
3 tablespoons flour	4 egg yolks
1½ cups hot milk	¾ to 1 cup grated Gruyere, Parmesan, or cheddar cheese
½ teaspoon salt	mesan, or cheddar cheese
pinch of cayenne pepper	5 egg whites

Preheat oven to 375° F.

Butter a 1-quart souffle dish or 4 1-cup ramekins. Sprinkle the inside with bread crumbs. Prepare collars if desired.

In a 1-quart saucepan, melt the butter, stir in the flour, and cook the roux until the mixture starts to turn golden. Stir in the milk and cook, stirring, until the mixture is thick and smooth. Stir in the salt, cayenne, and nutmeg. Reduce, stirring often, to 1 cup. Beat in the egg yolks, one at a time, and bring to a boil. Remove from the heat and stir in the cheese until melted.

Beat the egg whites until stiff, but not dry, and fold into the cheese mixture. Pour into a prepared souffle dish. Bake on lowest rack of the oven for 12 to 18 minutes for individual souffles, or 25 to 35 minutes for a 1-quart souffle.

Serves 4.

ROLLED CHEESE SOUFFLE

Butter an 11 by 17 inch jelly roll pan, line with waxed paper, and butter the paper. Sprinkle with bread crumbs. Spread the cheese souffle mixture in the bottom of the pan and bake for about 12 minutes, or until golden and just barely baked.

Place two sheets of waxed paper slightly overlapping on a work surface. Turn the souffle onto the waxed paper and peel off the bottom paper. Fill if desired, roll, and serve with a sauce. (For a filling use spinach or coarsely chopped cooked fresh tomatoes.)

Serves 4 to 6.

Souffle au Fromage aux Croutons d'Ail
(Cheese Souffle with Garlic Croutons)

1 recipe cheese souffle with Gruyere cheese	1 cup garlic croutons
	2 cups tomato sauce

Fold the croutons into the souffle mixture just before folding in the egg whites. Bake. Serve the sauce separately.

Serves 4.

CROUTONS D'AIL (GARLIC CROUTONS)

¼ cup butter	1 cup bread cubes, crusts removed
2 to 4 garlic cloves, split	

Melt the butter in a skillet and add the garlic. Cook over low heat until the garlic is golden brown, but not burned. Remove the garlic and saute the bread crumbs in the butter until golden.

Souffle de Choufleur (Cauliflower Souffle)

1 head cauliflower
salt and pepper to taste
1 teaspoon onion juice
2 tablespoons grated Parmesan
  cheese

8 anchovy fillets, minced
1 recipe cheese souffle, without
  cheese

Preheat oven to 375° F.
Prepare souffle dish and set aside.
Remove stems from cauliflower and break into florets. Steam over boiling salted water until very tender. Puree in a food mill or processor. Season the puree with salt, pepper, onion juice, cheese, and anchovy fillets. Add the puree to the Bechamel and egg yolk mixture. Fold in the egg whites and bake.
Serves 4 to 6.
Note: To remove the juice from an onion, cut in half horizontally. Using a lemon or orange juicer, ream out the juice from each onion half.

Souffle de Gourilos (Escarole Souffle)

1 head escarole, shredded
3 scallions, thinly sliced
3 tablespoons butter

½ teaspoon Worcestershire sauce
1 recipe cheese souffle with cheddar
  cheese

Preheat oven to 375° F.
Prepare souffle dish and set aside.
In a 3-quart saucepan of boiling salted water, blanch the escarole for 5 minutes. Drain and squeeze dry. In a 9-inch skillet, saute the scallions in the butter until soft. Add the escarole and cook, stirring, until the liquid has evaporated. Fold into the souffle mixture with the Worcestershire and cheddar. Finish as a regular souffle and bake.
Serves 4.

Souffle de Homard Plaza Athenee (Lobster Souffle)

1 2-pound live lobster	1 tablespoon cognac
1 tablespoon butter	½ cup dry white wine
1 tablespoon minced carrot	½ cup heavy cream
1 tablespoon minced celery	½ cup cream sauce
1 tablespoon minced chives	1½ tablespoons heavy cream
½ tablespoon minced parsley	1½ tablespoons dry sherry
salt and pepper to taste	1 recipe cheese souffle made with
¼ cup vegetable oil	half Parmesan and half Gruyere
½ teaspoon paprika	cheese

Preheat oven to 375° F.

Prepare a 1-quart souffle dish with a collar.

While the lobster is still alive, separate the tail and body with a heavy, sharp knife. Remove the claws from the lobster and chop each claw into 3 pieces. Chop the tail into 3 pieces. Chop the body in half lengthwise and crosswise into 4 sections.

In a small skillet, saute the carrot and celery in the butter until soft. Season with chives, parsley, salt, and pepper.

In a 12-inch skillet, heat the oil and saute the lobster, carrot mixture, and paprika until the lobster shell turns red. Stir in the cognac, wine, and ½ cup cream and simmer gently for 10 minutes. Remove the lobster from the sauce and take the meat from the shells. Cut into ¼-inch slices.

Reduce the sauce by half. Stir in the cream sauce, remaining cream, and sherry. Cook, stirring, 1 minute. Strain. Pour half of the sauce over the lobster and reserve the remainder. Place the lobster mixture in the bottom of the souffle dish. Prepare the souffle and pour over the lobster. Bake 35 to 40 minutes.

Heat the remaining sauce. Serve the souffle with the sauce on the side. Serves 4.

Note: This can also be prepared as a rolled souffle. The lobster sauce can be prepared several days ahead and reheated, or even frozen. It can also be served alone without its souffle topping.

Salmon and Broccoli Souffle

1 recipe cheese souffle made with 4 tablespoons grated Parmesan cheese	1 teaspoon minced dill
	10 ounces cooked broccoli, pureed
½ cup cooked, flaked salmon	¼ teaspoon nutmeg
1½ teaspoons tomato paste	2 tablespoons grated Parmesan cheese

Preheat oven to 375° F.

Prepare a 1-quart souffle dish.

Before folding the egg whites into the souffle base, divide the base into two parts. Combine the salmon, tomato paste, and dill with one part and the broccoli and nutmeg with the remaining base. Fold half of the beaten egg whites into each mixture.

Place the broccoli mixture in the bottom of the prepared souffle dish. Top with the salmon mixture. Sprinkle the two tablespoons of grated Parmesan over the top of the souffle. Bake for 35 to 40 minutes. Serve immediately.

Serves 4.

Souffle au Fromage et Jambon
(Souffle with Ham and Cheese)

1 recipe cheese souffle with Gruyere cheese	1 cup very finely diced ham
	2 tablespoons Dijon mustard

Prepare the souffle mixture except for folding in the egg whites. Fold the ham and mustard into the sauce base, then fold in the beaten egg whites. Bake as directed for cheese souffle.

Serves 4.

Souffle aux Crevettes a l'Estragon
(Shrimp Souffle with Tarragon)

4 tablespoons butter	⅓ cup dry white wine
2 tablespoons minced onion	1 pound shrimp, peeled and
1 tablespoon minced shallot	deveined
1 teaspoon minced garlic	cayenne pepper to taste
2 cups tomatoes, peeled, seeded, and chopped	2 tablespoons cognac
salt and pepper to taste	1 recipe cheese souffle made with half Parmesan and half Gruyere cheese
1½ tablespoons dried tarragon	
1 tablespoon minced parsley	Parmesan cheese

Preheat oven to 375° F.

Prepare a 1½-quart souffle dish.

In a 10-inch skillet, saute the onion, shallot, and garlic in 2 tablespoons of butter until soft. Add the tomatoes, salt, pepper, tarragon, and parsley. Simmer 5 minutes. Add the wine and simmer 15 minutes.

In a 9-inch skillet, saute the shrimp in the remaining butter with the cayenne. Correct seasoning. Add cognac and ignite, turning your face away. Add to the tomato sauce and correct the seasoning.

Prepare the souffle mixture. Put the sauce in the bottom of the souffle dish and top with the souffle. (Can be made as a rolled souffle and filled with the sauce mixture.) Bake as directed for cheese souffle. Serve sprinkled with Parmesan.

The sauce can be made several days before or even frozen.

Serves 6.

Roulade de Fromage au Coquilles St. Jacques (Cheese Roll with Scallop Sauce)

3 tablespoons butter	½ teaspoon dried oregano
2 tablespoons minced garlic	2 egg yolks
1½ pounds scallops	salt and pepper to taste
¼ cup dry white wine	2 tablespoons minced parsley
½ cup tomato sauce	1 recipe cheese souffle with Gruyere
1¼ cups heavy cream	cheese
1 teaspoon minced fresh basil	

Preheat oven to 375° F.

Prepare a jelly roll pan for rolled souffle (see page 88).

In a 9-inch skillet, melt the butter and saute the garlic for 1 minute, or until soft but not browned. Add the scallops and cook over high heat for about 1 minute, or until just barely under-cooked. With a slotted spoon, remove the scallops and set aside. Add the wine, tomato sauce, and 1 cup cream to the saucepan. Simmer 3 minutes. Stir in the basil and oregano.

In a bowl, combine the egg yolks and remaining cream. Stir some of the hot sauce into the egg yolk mixture to warm it. Then add egg mixture to the sauce. Heat until lightly thickened, but do not boil. Correct seasoning with salt and pepper. Return scallops to the sauce.

Prepare souffle mixture and bake as for a rolled souffle. Unmold, fill with some of scallop mixture, roll up, and place on a serving platter. Spoon remaining scallop mixture over souffle and serve immediately.

The sauce can be prepared ahead, but be careful not to overcook the scallops when you reheat the sauce.

Serves 6.

Note: The scallop sauce can be served as a crepe filling or alone.

Roulade de Jambon au Creme de Moutarde
(Ham Roll with Mustard Cream Sauce)

1 recipe cheese souffle
1 pound ham, finely ground
salt and pepper to taste
2 teaspoons dried tarragon
½ cup dry Madeira

1 cup sour cream
1 tablespoon Dijon mustard
1 teaspoon dried tarragon
2 tablespoons minced parsley

Preheat oven to 375° F.

Prepare a jelly roll pan for a rolled souffle.

To the sauce base for the souffle, add the ham, salt, pepper, 2 teaspoons tarragon, and Madeira. Mix well. Fold in the egg whites and spread the mixture in the prepared pan. Bake for 10 to 12 minutes, or until just set.

Meanwhile, combine the cream, mustard, remaining tarragon, and parsley in a saucepan. Mix well and heat without boiling. Unmold the souffle, roll up, and pour the sauce over the top.

Serves 4 to 6.

Roulade d'Epinards aux Champignons
(Rolled Souffle with Spinach and Mushrooms)

1 recipe basic souffle
2 pounds spinach, stripped,
  wilted, squeezed dry, and
  minced
1½ pounds mushrooms, minced

3 tablespoons butter
nutmeg, salt, and pepper to taste
¾ cup heavy cream
1 cup Hollandaise sauce

Preheat oven to 375° F.

Prepare a jelly roll pan for a rolled souffle.

Prepare the souffle mixture and fold the spinach into the sauce base before adding the egg whites. Bake 10 to 12 minutes until set.

Saute the mushrooms in the butter until the liquid has evaporated and season with nutmeg, salt, and pepper. Stir in the cream and simmer until thickened. Unmold the souffle, fill with mushroom mixture, and roll. Serve with Hollandaise sauce over the top.

Serves 6.

Note: You can substitute the mushrooms for the spinach in the souffle recipe and use the spinach in the filling.

DESSERT SOUFFLES

Sweet foods often are eaten at breakfasts and brunches, and you can serve a sweet souffle as a light dessert following a light meal. As with entree souffles, the basic recipe is much the same—a cream base with flavoring and egg white leavening. The principal difference is that you use more eggs and less sauce.

Souffle a la Vanille (Basic Vanilla Souffle)

½ cup milk	5 egg yolks
1-inch piece vanilla bean	3 tablespoons sugar
2 tablespoons butter	6 egg whites
1½ tablespoons flour	1 tablespoon sugar

Preheat oven to 425° F.

Butter and sugar a 1-quart souffle dish. Add a collar if desired.

In a small saucepan, scald the milk with the vanilla bean and let steep 10 minutes. In a medium saucepan, melt the butter, stir in the flour, and cook the roux until the mixture just starts to turn golden. Stir in the scalded milk and cook, stirring, until the mixture is thick and smooth. Simmer 5 minutes. Remove the vanilla bean.

In a small bowl, beat the egg yolks with 3 tablespoons of sugar until light. Beat into the sauce mixture. Beat the egg whites until stiff, adding the remaining tablespoon of sugar during the final minutes of beating. Fold into the egg yolk mixture and pour into the prepared souffle dish. Bake for 15 to 20 minutes. Serve immediately.

Serves 4 to 6.

CHOCOLATE SOUFFLE   Melt 1½ ounces of unsweetened chocolate with the milk. Use 5 tablespoons of sugar instead of 3 with the egg yolks.

COFFEE SOUFFLE   Beat 2 tablespoons of double-strength coffee into the sauce mixture.

ORANGE SOUFFLE   Omit the vanilla from the milk and add the grated rind of 1 orange. Beat 2 tablespoons orange juice and 1 tablespoon orange liqueur into the sauce mixture.

FRUIT-FLAVORED SOUFFLE   Add ½ cup pureed fruit to the sauce mixture and a complementary liqueur if desired before folding in egg whites. For example, add orange, raspberry, or kirsch to strawberry puree; rum, cognac, or kirsch to pineapple puree; and framboise to raspberry puree.

CHAPTER 5
Quiche

Perhaps no single dish has captured the American imagination as much as the quiche, a French import that became generally known after World War II. The quiche has become one of the most acceptable and readily available brunch dishes. It is so popular that some party-givers prepare tiny quiche to serve as hors d'oeuvre. However, there is usually more pastry than filling in a tiny quiche.

A quiche is a pie shell filled with flavoring ingredients, such as cheese, fish, and meat, held together with a custard. It can be made ahead and reheated although, as with so many baked products, it is best served fresh out of the oven. You can make individual quiche or you can make one as large as your oven can accommodate. Traditionally, they are 9-inch rounds, but if you are having a large group, you may prefer to make quiche in a deep-sided baking sheet and cut it into squares.

For those who regard the filling as the principal reason for a quiche, a deeper pan can be used. You can prepare the quiche in spring form pans 2 or 3 inches deep. The only change is in the length of baking time. The diet-conscious cook can prepare the various suggestions in this section without using pie shells. Refer to the section on baked eggs (chapter 3) to learn how to prepare these in a water bath.

THE PIE SHELL

A recipe for pie pastry appears on page 204. If you are short of time or unskilled at making pastry, the frozen, unbaked pie shells available in most markets are suitable.

If there are two crusts to the pie, or if it is deeper than 1½ inches, the pastry should be filled before baking. If the filling is exposed and less than 2 inches deep, the shell should be prebaked for about 15 minutes. Prebaking ensures that the shell will be fully cooked when the filling is baked. Some writers suggest brushing the shell with lightly beaten egg white to seal it before prebaking.

THE FILLING

You can use virtually anything in a custard to make a quiche filling. Some foods must be cooked before going into the shell since they will not cook in the shell with the custard. For example, smoked salmon (which is really raw fish) would not be precooked since it is eaten raw. Minced onions probably would be precooked as for other cooked dishes.

THE CUSTARD

There are no hard rules for the custard. Four egg yolks and 2 cups of cream are enough to fill a 9-inch shell holding about 1½ cups of filling. If you want a creamier, richer custard, add one or more extra egg yolks and use a heavier cream.

BAKING

Quiche bake at 375° F. to 400° F. for 35 to 55 minutes. For a deeper quiche, lower the temperature to 350° F. and bake for 60 minutes or longer. Do not try to rush the cooking of a quiche by raising the oven temperature. The eggs will harden and you will have a watery quiche instead of the preferred creamy custard. The quiche is cooked when a knife inserted halfway between the edge and the center is clean when removed. Allow the quiche to rest in a draft-free area for at least 10 minutes before serving. The rest allows the quiche to finish cooking and settle. It will not become cold unless the area is extremely cold.

FREEZING

Although there is no question that a freshly prepared quiche is the most delicious, you can freeze a quiche, if necessary. After the quiche is baked, cool and wrap securely in metal foil or another freezer wrap. Freeze as quickly as possible and keep as cold as possible. It will keep at its best for one month. To serve, unwrap the quiche and let thaw to room temperature. Reheat in a 350° F. oven until warm. *Do not* try to serve it very hot or the eggs will be overcooked.

Quiche Lorraine (Bacon and Cheese Custard)

6 slices bacon, cooked
6 ounces thinly sliced Gruyere
  cheese
1 9-inch pie shell, half baked
2 cups heavy cream

4 large eggs
salt, pepper, and nutmeg to
  taste
butter

Preheat oven to 375° F.

Arrange the bacon and cheese in the bottom of the pie shell. In a 2-quart bowl, beat the cream, eggs, salt, pepper, and nutmeg until well mixed. Pour into the shell and dot with butter. Bake for 35 to 40 minutes.

Serves 6.

Quiche au Homard (Lobster Quiche)

2 tablespoons minced shallots	4 eggs, well beaten
1½ tablespoons butter	1 teaspoon minced chives
½ pound lobster meat, cooked and diced	1 truffle, minced, optional
	salt and pepper to taste
2 tablespoons cognac	Tabasco sauce to taste
½ teaspoon dried tarragon	1 9-inch pie shell, half baked
2 cups heavy cream	

Preheat oven to 375° F.

In a 7-inch skillet, saute the shallots in the butter until soft. Stir in the lobster and heat. Sprinkle with cognac and tarragon and simmer 1 minute. Remove from heat. Blend in the cream, eggs, chives, truffle, salt, pepper, and Tabasco. Pour into the prepared shell. Bake for 35 to 40 minutes.

Serves 6.

Note: You may substitute shrimp, crab, or scallops for the lobster.

Salmon Quiche

2 tablespoons minced shallots	¼ cup liquid from poaching salmon
2 tablespoons butter	
1 pound salmon, poached, skinned, boned, and flaked	1 9-inch pie shell, half baked
	1 cup heavy cream
3 tablespoons minced dill	4 eggs, lightly beaten
salt and pepper to taste	

Preheat oven to 375° F.

In a 7-inch skillet, saute the shallots in the butter. Mix into the flaked salmon with the dill, salt, pepper, and poaching liquor. Put into the pie shell.

In a medium bowl, combine the cream and eggs and correct seasoning with salt and pepper. Pour into the shell and bake for 35 to 40 minutes.

Serves 6.

Mexican Custard Tart with Chilies and Cheese

1 tablespoon minced shallots
2 tablespoons butter
4 ounces green chilies, minced
1 9-inch pie shell, baked

2 cups grated cheddar cheese
4 large eggs, lightly beaten
1 cup heavy cream
½ teaspoon salt

Preheat oven to 375° F.

In a 7-inch skillet, saute the shallots in the butter until soft. Stir in the chilies and heat. Place in the pie shell and sprinkle with cheese.

In a medium bowl, combine the eggs, cream, and salt. Pour into the shell. Bake until set, about 35 to 40 minutes.

Serves 6.

Quiche Honfleuraise (Seafood Quiche)

3 pounds mussels, scrubbed and
　bearded
2 shallots, minced
2 onions, minced
¾ cup dry white wine
salt and pepper to taste
½ pint oysters

¼ pound shrimp, peeled and
　deveined
1 9-inch pie shell, half baked
1 cup heavy cream
4 eggs, lightly beaten
nutmeg to taste

Preheat oven to 375° F.

In a 3-quart casserole, combine the mussels, shallots, onions, wine, salt, and pepper. Cover and bring to a boil. Simmer 5 minutes. Strain and reserve the liquid. Remove the mussels from their shells and reserve the meat.

Poach the oysters in their own liquor and drain. Poach the shrimp in the strained mussel liquor. Place the mussels, oysters, and shrimp in the pie shell.

In a medium bowl, beat the cream, eggs, salt, pepper, and nutmeg. Add ½ cup mussel liquor and mix well. Pour into the shell and bake for 35 to 40 minutes, or until set.

Serves 6.

Italian Custard Pie

6 eggs
¼ cup milk
7 ounces tuna in oil, drained and
   flaked
½ pound grated mozzarella cheese

salt and pepper to taste
½ teaspoon dried basil
½ teaspoon dried oregano
1 9-inch pie shell, half baked

Preheat oven to 375° F.

In a bowl, beat the eggs and milk until blended. Stir in the tuna, cheese, salt, pepper, basil, and oregano. Pour into the shell. Bake for 35 to 40 minutes, or until set.

Serves 6.

Beef and Tomato Quiche

1 bunch scallions, thinly sliced
2 tablespoons butter
1 pound lean ground beef
1 large tomato, peeled, seeded, and
   chopped
1½ teaspoons salt
½ teaspoon dried marjoram

½ teaspoon dried thyme
½ teaspoon pepper
1½ cups heavy cream
4 eggs, lightly beaten
1 9-inch pie shell, half baked
1 tablespoon minced parsley

Preheat oven to 375° F.

In a 9-inch skillet, saute the scallions in the butter until soft. Add the beef and cook, breaking it up, until it loses its color. Stir in the tomato, salt, marjoram, thyme, and pepper. Simmer 5 minutes.

In a medium bowl, beat the cream and eggs together. Add the meat mixture and pour into the shell. Bake for 35 to 40 minutes, or until set.

Serves 6.

Artichoke and Sausage Deep Custard Pie

½ cup scallions, minced
1 tablespoon butter
10 ounces cooked artichoke hearts
4 eggs, lightly beaten
1 pound ricotta cheese
½ cup sour cream
2 ounces grated Parmesan cheese
4 ounces grated Gruyere cheese

3 ounces ham in julienne
⅓ cup minced parsley
¾ pound mild Italian sausage, cooked, peeled, and thinly sliced
salt and pepper to taste
1 10-inch spring form pan, lined with pie pastry (see p. 204)

Preheat oven to 425° F.

In a 9-inch skillet, saute the scallions in the butter. Add the artichokes and heat.

In a medium bowl, beat the eggs, ricotta, and sour cream until well blended. Stir in the Parmesan, Gruyere, ham, parsley, sausage, scallions, and artichokes. Correct seasoning with salt and pepper. Pour into pastry. Bake 10 minutes.

Lower the heat to 375° F. and bake 50 minutes. Cool in the pan for 10 minutes, remove the sides, and serve warm.

Serves 6 to 8.

Mushroom, Onion, and Sausage Quiche

½ pound sliced onions
2 tablespoons bacon fat
2 eggs
2 egg yolks
2 teaspoons Dijon mustard
½ cup grated Parmesan cheese
1¼ cups light cream

½ pound sliced mushrooms
2 tablespoons butter
1 tablespoon lemon juice
salt and pepper to taste
½ pound sausage meat, cooked and crumbled
1 9-inch pie shell, half baked

Preheat oven to 375° F.

In a 7-inch skillet, saute the onions in the bacon fat until soft, but not brown.

In a medium bowl, beat the eggs, egg yolks, mustard, Parmesan, and cream. Stir in the onion.

In a 9-inch skillet, saute the mushrooms in the butter and lemon juice until soft. Correct seasoning with salt and pepper. Add to the custard with the sausage and pour into the pie shell. Bake for 35 to 40 minutes, or until set.

Serves 6.

Zucchini and Ham Quiche

¼ cup minced onion	4 large eggs
1 small clove garlic, minced	¾ cup milk
2 tablespoons butter	½ cup heavy cream
salt and pepper to taste	1 9-inch pie shell, half baked
1¼ pounds zucchini, thinly sliced	¼ cup grated Parmesan cheese
¼ pound sliced boiled ham, minced	

Preheat oven to 375° F.

In a 9-inch skillet, saute the onion and garlic in the butter until soft, but not brown. Add the salt, pepper, and zucchini and cook until tender. Stir in the ham.

In a medium bowl, beat the eggs, milk, and cream together. Correct seasoning. Stir in the zucchini mixture. Pour into the pie shell. Sprinkle with cheese. Bake for 35 to 40 minutes, or until set.

Serves 6.

CHAPTER 6
Crepes

Like quiche, crepes have become a particular favorite of many cooks and party-givers. They are simple to make and freeze beautifully. They can be thawed, filled, and served with a few moments notice. Being rather bland tasting, crepes make perfect containers for flavorful fillings.

The number of crepes to serve each guest depends on the extent of the menu and on the heartiness of the filling. Although the crepe itself is light and delicate, the fillings are often substantial.

A definite advantage to serving crepes for breakfasts and brunches is that they cannot only be cooked and frozen well ahead of time, but also they can be filled and kept in the refrigerator until it is time to reheat them. They almost always are reheated before serving. Remember, if you are delayed in serving, it is better to let food cool and reheat it, rather than try to keep it hot.

Crepes can be assembled in several different ways. Usually, the filling is placed on the crepe and it is rolled into a tube, laid in a baking dish, and coated with a sauce. However, crepes also can be folded into quarters with the filling put in one section, or even stacked like a cake. Make your own choice regarding the presentation.

ADDITIONAL FILLINGS FOR CREPES

In addition to the crepe fillings given in this section, you can fill crepes with souffle mixtures found in chapter 4. You can also use the lobster, shrimp, or scallop sauce recipes from the same chapter, or some of the mixtures mentioned in other chapters.

Entree Crepes

3 eggs	4 tablespoons melted butter
¾ cup sifted flour	½ teaspoon salt
1 cup milk	1 teaspoon cognac

Using a medium bowl, gradually work the eggs into the flour to form a thick paste. Slowly add the milk, stirring constantly to remove any lumps. The mixture will get very thick, then paste-like, and finally like heavy cream. Do not rush this step. Add the butter, salt, and cognac. Strain the mixture and let rest in a draft-free area for 2 hours. The batter should be the consistency of heavy cream. If necessary, thin with milk.

You can make the crepes by putting all of the ingredients in a blender or food processor and blending until smooth. This process eliminates the need to rest the batter.

Yields about 18 crepes.

COOKING CREPES

You can use a steel crepe pan with a 7-inch bottom, or an aluminum or non-stick omelet pan to cook crepes. Put about 2 teaspoons of butter into the pan. Melt the butter over medium heat until it begins to smell nutty. Pour the excess butter into the batter. With a ladle, scoop about 3 tablespoons of batter into the pan and swirl the pan to cover the bottom completely. Place over heat and cook until golden brown on the bottom. With a supple metal spatula, carefully lift the crepe, flip it over, and cook until golden. Turn out onto a sheet of foil or waxed paper. Continue with remaining batter.

It should not be necessary to butter the pan more than once or twice during the entire cooking procedure. With practice, you should be able to work two pans at once to complete the job quickly.

Stack the cooked crepes in groups of 12 to 16, wrap them securely in foil, and freeze for up to two months. They can be stored in the refrigerator for 3 days before filling.

Dessert Crepes

⅔ cup flour	2 egg yolks
1 tablespoon sugar	1¾ cups milk
pinch of salt	2 tablespoons melted butter
2 whole eggs	1 tablespoon rum or cognac

In a bowl, combine the flour, sugar, and salt. Make a well in the center and add the eggs and egg yolks. Mix into the flour completely to make a thick paste. Very gradually work in the milk to make a smooth batter. Add the butter and liqueur and let the batter rest for 2 hours. Strain before using.

These crepes also can be made in a blender or processor. Cook as directed.

Yields about 24 crepes.

Note: Dessert crepes are even more delicate than entree crepes. The first few crepes may tear, but persistance will be rewarded.

Gateau de Crepes aux Champignons
(Cake of Mushroom-Filled Crepes)

12 entree crepes
1½ cups duxelles (see Appendix)
2 cups grated Gruyere cheese

2½ cups hot Bechamel sauce
½ cup heavy cream

Preheat the oven to 425° F.

On an ovenproof serving platter, place a crepe and spread it with a layer of duxelles. Cover with another crepe. In a saucepan, combine the cheese and Bechamel. Spread about 1 tablespoon on the crepe. Keep layering the crepes, alternating the duxelles and Bechamel. Finish with a crepe.

Add the cream to the remaining Bechamel and pour over the top of the cake. Bake for 10 minutes, or until lightly browned on top and sizzling hot. If any ingredients were refrigerated overnight, reheat them before assembling.

The crepes, duxelles, and Bechamel can be frozen.

Serves 6.

Mushroom and Watercress Crepes

2 pounds mushrooms, thinly sliced
½ cup butter
½ cup minced onion
½ teaspoon salt
2 tablespoons flour

½ cup dry white wine
2 cups sour cream
3 cups watercress leaves
½ teaspoon Worcestershire sauce
16 entree crepes

In a 12-inch skillet, saute the mushrooms in the butter with the onion and salt until soft, but not brown. Stir in the flour and cook, stirring, for 5 minutes. Add the wine and cook until thickened. Remove from the heat and stir in the sour cream, watercress, and Worcestershire. Correct seasoning with salt and pepper. Fill crepes and arrange in a buttered baking dish. Serve immediately, or reheat at 350° F.

Filling can be made the day before and reheated in a saucepan before filling the crepes.

Serves 6 to 8.

Spinach and Dill Crepes

½ cup minced scallion
¾ cup butter
  2 pounds spinach, wilted and finely
    chopped
salt and pepper to taste
  2 tablespoons minced fresh dill
  1 large clove garlic, crushed

  1 cup sour cream
14 entree crepes, flavored with
    1 tablespoon minced dill
  3 tablespoons grated Parmesan
    cheese
  2 cups sour cream, optional

Preheat oven to 325° F.

In a 9-inch skillet, saute the scallion in 4 tablespoons butter until soft. Add the spinach and cook until heated through. Correct seasoning, and stir in the dill, garlic, and 3 tablespoons sour cream. Cook, stirring, until the liquid has evaporated. Remove from the heat and fold in the remaining sour cream.

Melt remaining butter. Fill the crepes and roll. Arrange in a baking dish and pour on the melted butter. Dust with Parmesan. Heat. Serve sour cream on the side, if desired.

Can be prepared the day before and heated, covered, in the oven until hot.

Serves 6 to 8.

Crespolini (Italian Crepes)

1 pound spinach, cooked and
  minced
1 cup ricotta cheese
2 eggs, lightly beaten
2 tablespoons grated Parmesan
  cheese

16 entree crepes
  1 cup thin cream sauce (see
    Appendix)
  1 cup grated Italian fontina
    cheese

Preheat oven to 325° F.

In a bowl, combine the spinach, ricotta, eggs, and Parmesan. Fill crepes, roll, and place in an ovenproof baking dish. Cover with cream sauce and sprinkle with grated fontina. Bake until bubbling and lightly browned.

Can be prepared for baking the day before.

Serves 6 to 8.

Crepes with Smoked Salmon

8 ounces softened cream cheese
1 cup sour cream
salt and pepper to taste
2 tablespoons minced dill

¼ pound minced smoked salmon
12 to 16 entree crepes, made with
  1 tablespoon minced dill
1 cup melted butter

Preheat oven to 325° F.

In a bowl, mix the cheese and sour cream until smooth. Beat in the salt, pepper, and dill. Fold in the salmon. Fill crepes, place in a baking dish, and pour on the butter. Heat until warm.

Can be prepared for reheating the night before.

Serves 6 to 8.

Crepes Farcis a la Monegasque (Stuffed Crepes Monaco)

¾ cup butter
4 anchovy fillets, minced
½ cup minced onions
2 cloves garlic, minced
3 tablespoons olive oil
5 tomatoes, peeled, seeded, and
  chopped

1 teaspoon oregano
salt and pepper to taste
6 stuffed olives, thinly sliced
1 cup minced pimiento
¾ pound cooked shrimp, diced
16 entree crepes

Preheat oven to 325° F.

In a small saucepan, heat the butter and anchovies until the anchovies dissolve.

In a 9-inch skillet, saute the onion and garlic in the oil until lightly browned. Add tomatoes, oregano, salt, and pepper. Simmer until thickened, about 20 minutes. Add olives, pimiento, and shrimp and heat. Correct seasoning with salt and pepper. Fill crepes and arrange in an ovenproof baking dish. Drizzle the anchovy butter over the crepes and reheat.

Can be prepared for reheating the night before.

Serves 6 to 8.

Crepes HRH Prince Bertil

1 pound cooked medium shrimp	16 entree crepes
¼ cup minced dill	8 tablespoons melted butter
¾ cup Hollandaise	4 tablespoons grated Parmesan
salt and pepper to taste	cheese

Preheat the oven to 350° F.

Combine the shrimp, dill, and Hollandaise. Correct the seasoning with salt and pepper. Fill crepes and arrange in an ovenproof serving dish. Drizzle melted butter over the crepes and sprinkle with the cheese. Heat until hot, then put under a broiler until golden brown.

Because of the delicacy of the Hollandaise, these should be assembled just before heating.

Serves 6 to 8.

Seafood Crepes, Brandy's

2 cups dry white wine	½ pound scallops
2 cups water	½ pound king crab, bite-size
½ cup chopped mushroom stems	pieces
¼ cup minced onion	3 tablespoons butter
1 bay leaf	3 tablespoons flour
2 teaspoons cognac	salt and pepper to taste
½ pound shrimp, peeled and	1 cup heavy cream
deveined	16 entree crepes

Preheat broiler.

In a 2-quart saucepan, combine the wine, water, mushrooms, onion, bay leaf, and cognac. Simmer until reduced to 2 cups. Strain. (This is a white wine court bouillon.) Poach the shrimp and scallops separately in the poaching liquor. Set the fish aside and strain the stock. Add crabmeat to the fish.

In a 1-quart saucepan, melt the butter, stir in the flour, and cook until the mixture starts to turn golden. Add the poaching liquor and cook, stirring, until thickened and smooth. Correct seasoning with salt and pepper. Add cream and simmer until reduced by one third. Set aside half of the sauce and fold the remainder into the fish.

Fill crepes, roll, and place in an ovenproof serving dish. Pour remaining sauce over the crepes. Glaze under the broiler.

Can be prepared for baking the day before. Reheat at 350° F. until bubbling hot. Glaze if needed.

Serves 6 to 8.

Curried Chicken-Filled Crepes with Chutney

¾ cup butter	2 cups chicken stock
2 cups minced onions	1 cup light cream
½ cup minced carrots	1 cup unsweetened coconut milk
½ cup minced celery	2 cups poached chicken, cubed
1 apple, chopped	¼ cup minced mango chutney
3 to 4 tablespoons curry powder	16 entree crepes
3 tablespoons flour	

Preheat oven to 350° F.

In a 2-quart saucepan, melt the butter and saute the onions, carrots, celery, and apple until soft, but not brown. Stir in the curry powder and flour and cook 2 minutes, stirring. Stir in the chicken stock and simmer 15 minutes. Add the cream and coconut milk and simmer 5 minutes.

Force the mixture through a sieve or puree in a processor. Fold half of the sauce into the chicken with the chutney. Fill crepes with the chicken mixture and arrange in an ovenproof serving dish. Spoon remaining sauce over the top. Heat until piping hot.

Can be prepared for heating the night before.

Serves 6 to 8.

Crepes Nicoise (Crepes Nice-Style)

1 cup ground lean veal	¾ cup heavy cream
1 cup ground lean pork	12 entree crepes
¼ cup minced shallots	1 cup thinly sliced mushrooms
1 tablespoon minced parsley	juice of 1 lemon
dash of cayenne pepper	2 cups warm Bechamel sauce
salt and pepper to taste	grated Parmesan or Gruyere
3 tablespoons butter	cheese
1 tablespoon flour	

Preheat broiler.

In a 12-inch skillet, saute the veal, pork, shallots, parsley, cayenne, salt, and pepper in the butter until the meats lose their color and start to brown.

Sprinkle with flour and cook, stirring, for 3 minutes. Add the cream and cook, stirring, until lightly thickened. Fill the crepes with the mixture and arrange in an ovenproof serving dish.

In a 1-quart saucepan, combine the mushrooms and lemon juice with enough water to cover. Simmer 10 minutes. Strain and stir the mushrooms into the Bechamel. Pour over the crepes and sprinkle with the cheese. Glaze under the broiler.

Can be prepared the night before and reheated at 350° F.

Serves 6.

Crepes au Jambon et Fromage (Ham and Cheese Crepes)

16 slices lean ham	¼ cup cognac
16 slices Gruyere cheese	salt and pepper to taste
16 entree crepes	grated Parmesan cheese
4 cups Bechamel	paprika

Preheat oven to 350° F.

Roll a slice of ham and cheese in each crepe and arrange in an oven-proof serving dish. In a saucepan, combine the Bechamel and cognac and simmer 5 minutes. Correct the seasoning with salt and pepper. Pour over crepes and sprinkle with cheese and paprika. Heat until bubbling.

Can be prepared for baking the day before.

Serves 6 to 8.

Crepes Favorites

2 sweet red peppers, diced	salt and pepper to taste
1 pound sweetbreads, blanched and diced	lemon juice to taste
½ cup diced ham	16 crepes
4 tablespoons butter	½ cup melted butter
2 cups chicken veloute	grated Parmesan cheese

Preheat oven to 350° F.

In a 9-inch skillet, saute the peppers, sweetbreads, and ham in 2 table-spoons of butter. Add the veloute and simmer 5 minutes. Correct seasoning with salt, pepper, and lemon juice. Fill crepes, roll, and arrange in an ovenproof serving dish. Melt remaining butter, pour on, and sprinkle with the cheese. Heat in the oven.

Can be prepared the night before. Cover with foil and reheat.

Serves 6 to 8.

Crepazes (Cake of Ham, Cheese, and Crepes)

1 cup heavy cream
salt and pepper to taste
10 entree crepes
6 ounces thinly sliced prosciutto
or Westphalian ham

6 ounces thinly sliced Virginia ham
2 ounces grated Gruyere cheese

Preheat oven to 350° F.

In a small saucepan, heat the cream with the salt and pepper until hot, but not boiling. Lightly butter a charlotte mold or ¾-quart souffle dish. Cut crepes to fit the dish. Place a crepe in the bottom and top with a slice of prosciutto and a tablespoon of cream. Keep layering, alternating slices of the ham as you proceed. The top layer should be a crepe.

Heat in the oven until very hot. Unmold and sprinkle with cheese. Place under the broiler until the cheese is melted and lightly browned. Serve cut into wedges.

Can be prepared for baking the night before.

Serves 4 to 6.

Crepes Farcies Provencale (Crepes Provence-Style)

¾ cup olive oil
1 large eggplant, cubed
2 zucchini, diced
3 onions, thinly sliced
1 green pepper, thinly sliced
1 red pepper, thinly sliced
4 tomatoes, peeled, seeded, and chopped
1 teaspoon dried basil

½ teaspoon dried oregano
2 tablespoons minced parsley
2 cloves garlic, minced
salt and pepper to taste
16 entree crepes
16 slices prosciutto
¾ cup melted butter
½ cup grated Parmesan cheese

Preheat the oven to 350° F.

In a large skillet, saute the eggplant in ½ cup olive oil until browned.

Remove to a bowl. Saute the zucchini in the remaining oil until browned. Add the onions, peppers, and tomatoes to the skillet and simmer until the juices have evaporated. Season with basil, oregano, parsley, garlic, salt, and pepper. Return eggplant to the skillet mixture and cook 5 minutes, or until tender.

Line each crepe with a slice of prosciutto and fill with vegetable mixture. Roll and arrange in an ovenproof baking dish. Drizzle with butter and sprinkle with the cheese. Reheat.

Can be prepared for baking the day before.

Serves 6 to 8.

Gateau de Crepes aux Abricots (Cake of Crepes and Apricots)

1½ cups stewed apricots
2 tablespoons rum
sugar to taste

12 dessert crepes
1 cup sour cream

Preheat oven to 350° F.

In a bowl, combine the apricots with rum and sugar. Spread a thin layer on each crepe, and stack into a cake on an ovenproof serving dish. Cover with foil and heat. Serve cut in wedges, with sour cream on the side.

Can be prepared for baking the day before.

Serves 6 to 8.

Crepes aux Pommes (Crepes Filled with Apples and Cream)

3 apples, peeled and cored
6 tablespoons butter
juice of ½ lemon
5 tablespoons apricot jam
5 tablespoons chopped almonds

½ cup heavy cream, whipped
4 tablespoons Calvados
12 to 16 dessert crepes
½ cup crushed macaroons
2 to 3 tablespoons sugar

Preheat broiler.

In a 9-inch skillet, saute the apples in 5 tablespoons butter and the lemon juice until soft. Stir in the apricot jam and almonds. Cool. Fold the cream into the apple mixture with the Calvados (applejack). Fill crepes and fold into quarters. Arrange on an ovenproof serving dish and sprinkle with macaroons and sugar. Add remaining butter. Glaze under the broiler.

Assemble shortly before serving.

Serves 6 to 8.

Gateau de Crepes a la Normande (Normandy Apple Cake)

4 to 5 cups sliced apples	6 to 8 macaroons, crushed
⅓ cup sugar	4 tablespoons melted butter
4 tablespoons melted butter	4 tablespoons sugar
12 dessert crepes	4 tablespoons Cointreau

Preheat oven to 350° F.

Spread the apples in a baking pan and sprinkle with ⅓ cup sugar and 4 tablespoons butter. Bake for 15 minutes, or until apples are tender.

In a buttered ovenproof serving dish, place a crepe and spread with a thin layer of apple. Sprinkle lightly with macaroon crumbs, a few drops of butter, sugar, and Cointreau. Continue making layers, ending with a crepe. Sprinkle the top with the remaining butter and sugar. Increase heat in oven to 375° F. and bake the cake for 30 minutes, or until bubbling hot.

Can be prepared for baking the day before. Cover with foil and heat for 15 minutes.

Serves 6 to 8.

Crepes aux Fraises (Strawberry Crepes)

½ pint strawberries, sliced	½ cup heavy cream
¼ cup sugar	12 dessert crepes
3 tablespoons butter	3 tablespoons sugar
2 tablespoons orange liqueur	

Preheat broiler.

In a bowl, toss the strawberries with ¼ cup sugar. Melt the butter in a 9-inch skillet and immediately saute the strawberries over high heat until the sugar begins to caramelize. Add the liqueur and cream and cook over high heat until reduced by ¼. Fill crepes and pour remaining pan juices over them. Sprinkle with sugar and glaze.

Prepare just before serving.

Serves 4 to 6.

Crepe Souffle au Cointreau (Souffleed Crepes with Cointreau)

1 recipe dessert crepes
1 recipe orange souffle (see page 96)

granulated sugar
3 tablespoons Cointreau

Preheat oven to 400° F.

Prepare crepes ahead. Make orange souffle mixture. Fill crepes and fold into quarters. Place on a buttered ovenproof serving dish. Sprinkle with granulated sugar. Bake for 10 minutes, or until puffed and golden. Warm the Cointreau and ignite. Pour over the souffles and serve immediately.

Serves 6 to 8.

CHAPTER 7
Fish

Almost any fish dish is suitable for breakfast or brunch. Many preparations that usually take second place on a dinner menu are the stars at a brunch. The appetizers given in chapter 2 need only be prepared in larger quantities to serve as main courses. Recipes for fish served in cream sauces, mousses, or pies are also appropriate. Many of these can be prepared ahead and need only brief reheating. Quickly sauteed or deep fried, fish is a delicious change from the usual.

Keep in mind that the fish must be fresh and it must not be overcooked— undercook it slightly rather than overcook it. Read the recipes carefully to determine how much work can be done ahead of time; you will not have time for long, tedious preparations before an early brunch.

Although some of the dishes in this chapter can be frozen, most should be served immediately. However, much of the preparation can be done a day or so before. If a prepared dish has been frozen or refrigerated, let it come to room temperature before trying to reheat it. Even cold dishes taste best just below room temperature, rather than direct from the refrigerator. If you take a dish from the refrigerator to the oven, it is apt to be over-cooked along the edges and still cold in the center. Letting a dish sit out for an hour or so makes it possible to reheat it evenly. Remember, once food has been reheated, remove it from the heat. Do not try to keep it warm but reheat it again, if necessary.

SAUTEED FISH

For brunch or breakfast, select small fish such as trout or smelts, fish steaks such as salmon or haddock, or fillets of sole or cod.

Basic Sauteed Fish Recipe

1 cup flour	4 to 6 tablespoons clarified butter
1 teaspoon salt	4 tablespoons butter, optional
1/8 teaspoon pepper	1 to 2 tablespoons lemon juice
1 to 2 pounds fish	1 tablespoon minced parsley

In a plastic bag, combine the flour, salt, and pepper. Mix well. Toss the fish in the flour to coat lightly and shake off the excess. In a skillet large

117

enough to hold the fish in one layer, heat just enough clarified butter to coat the bottom of the pan until hot, but not smoking. Saute the fish until golden on both sides and just cooked. Remove to a serving platter.

If the butter is burned, pour it off and replace with fresh butter. If it is not burned, do not add any more. When the fresh butter is melted, add the lemon juice and parsley. Cook about 30 seconds and pour over the fish. Serve immediately. Do not try to cook ahead.

Serves 4.

Note: Allow about ¼ pound of fish fillet per person, or ½ pound of whole fish. A good rule of thumb is to cook fish 10 minutes per inch of thickness; for example, a ¼-inch thick fillet in 2½ minutes, a ½-inch steak in 5, and a 1-inch thick whole fish in 10 minutes.

DEEP-FRIED FISH

Select small whole fish such as smelts, or cut fillets of fish into *goujons* or fingers. They should measure about ½ inch by ½ inch by 3 inches.

Basic Fried Fish Recipe

1 quart oil for deep frying	⅛ teaspoon pepper
1 cup flour	1 pound fish
1 teaspoon salt	lemon wedges

In a 2-quart saucepan, heat 1 quart of oil to 375° F. In a plastic bag, combine flour, salt, and pepper. Mix well. Toss the fish in the flour to coat lightly and shake off the excess. Immediately deep fry until golden. Drain on paper toweling. Serve immediately with lemon wedges on the side. Do not try to cook ahead.

Serves 4.

Baked Avocado with Crab Aurore

4 tablespoons tomato puree	1 pound cooked crabmeat
2 tablespoons grated onion	3 ripe avocados, peeled
2 tablespoons butter	salt to taste
2 tablespoons curry powder	juice of 1 lemon
2 cups Bechamel sauce	

Preheat oven to 350° F.

In a 1½-quart bowl, combine the tomato puree, onion, butter, curry powder, Bechamel, and crabmeat. Mix well. Halve the avocados, remove the pits, and lightly score the flesh with the point of a small knife. Season with salt and lemon juice. Fill avocados with crab mixture and arrange in a baking dish. Add 1 inch of boiling water to the dish and bake for 20 minutes, or until tender.

The crab mixture can be prepared the day before. Do not fill avocados until shortly before baking.

Serves 6.

Crabe a la Diable (Deviled Crab)

2 cups picked-over crabmeat	salt and pepper to taste
2 tablespoons butter	½ cup heavy cream
2 cups Mornay sauce	4 tablespoons grated Parmesan
1 teaspoon dry mustard	cheese

Preheat broiler.

In a 9-inch skillet, saute the crabmeat in the butter until hot. Stir in 1 cup Mornay.

In a small bowl, combine the mustard and 3 tablespoons cold water. Stir into the crab mixture, mix well, and correct seasoning with salt and pepper. Arrange crab in individual baking dishes, one large baking dish, or scallop shells. Combine the cream and remaining Mornay and coat the crabmeat. Sprinkle with the cheese and glaze under the broiler.

Can be prepared the night before and reheated at 350° F. until bubbling hot.

Serves 4 to 6.

Crabmeat Tetrazzini

1 teaspoon minced shallots	1 cup cream sauce
2 tablespoons butter	1 to 2 tablespoons dry sherry
½ pound crabmeat	1 egg yolk
1 teaspoon paprika	1 pound thin spaghetti, cooked

In a 9-inch skillet, saute the shallots in the butter until soft. Stir in the crabmeat and heat. Stir in the paprika.

In a 1-quart saucepan, bring the cream sauce to a boil. Stir in the sherry and remove from the heat. Mix 3 tablespoons of the hot sauce into the egg yolk, then return it to the sauce. Put over heat and cook, stirring, until almost boiling. Do not boil. Stir the sauce into the crab mixture and serve over the spaghetti.

The crab mixture can be made the day before, but reheat it very gently or the sauce will curdle. The spaghetti should be cooked just before serving.

Serves 4 to 6.

Clam Pie

pastry for a 2-crust, 9-inch pie
 1 tablespoon minced parsley
¼ cup minced onions
 3 tablespoons butter
 3 tablespoons flour

 1 cup heavy cream
½ cup clam juice
 3 cups minced clams
 1 egg yolk
 1 tablespoon heavy cream

Preheat the oven to 425° F.

Line a 9-inch pie plate with pastry and sprinkle with the parsley.

In a 1-quart saucepan, saute the onion in the butter until soft, but not brown. Add the flour and cook the roux until it starts to turn golden. Stir in the cream and clam juice and cook, stirring, until the sauce comes to a boil and is thick and smooth.

Spread a layer of the clams in the pie shell and add a layer of sauce. Continue layering the ingredients. Roll the remaining pastry and cover the top of the pie. Cut a hole to let steam escape.

In a small bowl, combine the egg yolk and cream and brush over the pastry. Bake for 40 minutes, or until the pastry is golden brown.

Can be frozen and baked or reheated after freezing.

Serves 6 to 8.

Mussels in Mustard Cream

4 tablespoons butter
4 tablespoons minced shallots
1 teaspoon minced garlic
2 quarts mussels, scrubbed and
   bearded

pepper to taste
1 cup heavy cream
2 tablespoons Dijon mustard

In a 3-quart casserole, melt the butter. Stir in the shallots, garlic, mussels, and pepper. Cover and bring to a simmer. Add the cream and cook until the mussels start to open. Uncover, stir, cover, and simmer until all the mussels have opened. Transfer mussels to soup bowls.

Stir the mustard into the poaching liquor and strain over the mussels. Serve at once.

Do not prepare ahead.

Serves 4.

Scalloped Oysters

½ cup cracker crumbs	salt and pepper to taste
1 cup fresh bread crumbs	pinch of nutmeg
½ cup melted butter	4 tablespoons oyster liquor
1 pint oysters	2 tablespoons heavy cream

Preheat oven to 400° F.

In a bowl, combine the cracker and bread crumbs with the butter. Place a thin layer in the bottom of an 8 by 11 inch ovenproof serving dish. Cover with a layer of oysters, and season with salt, pepper, and nutmeg. Sprinkle on half of the oyster liquor and the cream. Make another layer of crumbs, oysters, seasonings, and liquids. Make a final layer of crumbs. Do not make more than 2 layers of the oysters or they will not cook properly. Bake for 30 minutes.

Can be prepared for baking the night before.

Serves 4.

Oyster Pie

sour cream pastry (see Appendix)	½ teaspoon cayenne pepper
4 slices bacon	1 quart oysters, drained
¼ cup minced onions	1 egg yolk mixed with 1 table-
½ cup minced scallions	spoon cream
¼ cup minced parsley	

Preheat oven to 425° F.

Prepare pastry and set aside.

In a 9-inch skillet, saute the bacon until crisp. Remove, drain, and break into bits. In the bacon fat, saute the onion until soft, but not brown.

In a bowl, combine the onion, bacon, scallions, parsley, and cayenne. Mix in the oysters. Butter 6 individual ramekins and divide the oyster mixture among them.

Roll the pastry ⅓ inch thick and cut out 6 circles large enough to cover the ramekins. Place over the bowls and crimp the edges. With the point of a sharp knife, score the surface of the pastry and pierce a hole to let the steam escape. Brush tops with egg yolk-cream mixture. Bake for 25 to 30 minutes, or until the dough is puffed and browned.

Can be prepared for baking the night before and kept in the refrigerator.

Serves 6.

Broiled Marinated Scallops

2 pounds scallops	1 teaspoon dried tarragon
1 cup olive oil	salt and pepper to taste
1 cup dry white wine	½ cup minced parsley
1 clove garlic, minced	lemon wedges

Rinse the scallops under cold running water and drain. In a large bowl, combine the oil, wine, garlic, tarragon, salt, pepper, and parsley. Add the scallops and marinate at room temperature for 2 hours. Thread the scallops onto skewers and broil until just cooked. Serve with lemon wedges.

Can be marinated overnight.

Serves 6 to 8.

Coquilles St. Jacques au Gratin
(Scallops with Mushroom Duxelles)

2 cups white wine court bouillon (see recipe for Seafood Crepes, Brandy's)	salt and pepper to taste
	2 cups duxelles (see Appendix)
2 pounds scallops	1 cup buttered bread crumbs
	minced parsley

Preheat the broiler.

Poach the scallops in the court bouillon and drain. If the scallops are large, cut into thick slices. Season with salt and pepper. Arrange scallops in individual serving dishes and coat with the duxelles. Sprinkle with bread crumbs and glaze under the broiler. Serve sprinkled with the minced parsley.

Can be prepared the night before and reheated at 350° F.

Serves 6 to 8.

Scallops Provencale with Spinach Noodles

1 pint scallops	¾ cup flour
¼ cup milk	½ cup olive oil
1½ pounds tomatoes, peeled, seeded, and chopped	1 tablespoon minced garlic
	3 tablespoons butter
1 bay leaf	½ pound spinach noodles, cooked
salt and pepper to taste	2 tablespoons minced parsley

Place scallops in a bowl, add the milk, and set aside.

Put tomatoes in a 9-inch skillet and bring to a boil. Set a sieve over a bowl and pour in the tomatoes. Drain for 5 minutes. Put the drained juice into a saucepan and reduce by half. Add the tomato pulp, bay leaf, salt, and pepper and simmer 3 minutes.

Drain the scallops and toss in the flour. Heat the oil in a 9-inch skillet until very hot and saute the scallops until golden. It is more important not to overcook the scallops than to brown them. Add the scallops to the tomato sauce.

In a small skillet, saute the garlic in the butter until golden, but not burned. Combine the noodles, scallops, and tomato sauce. Pour the garlic butter and parsley over all and serve.

The tomato sauce and the garlic butter can be made the night before.

Serves 4.

Mousse de Coquilles St. Jacques (Scallop Mousse)

4 cups fresh scallops	2 egg yolks
2 tablespoons butter	2 cups heavy cream
1 tablespoon minced shallots	tomato mushroom cream sauce
salt and pepper to taste	(recipe follows)
½ cup dry white wine	2 tablespoons minced parsley
nutmeg to taste	

Preheat oven to 375° F.

Set aside one cup of scallops. If they are large, cut into ½-inch cubes.

In a 9-inch skillet, saute the shallots in 1 tablespoon butter until soft, but not brown. Add the cup of scallops and season with salt and pepper. Cook until barely firm. Add the wine and cook 1 minute. Remove the scallops with a slotted spoon. Reserve the liquid in the skillet to use in the sauce.

In a processor, puree half of the raw scallops and add salt, pepper, and nutmeg to taste. Add one egg yolk and process until well blended. Stop to scrape down several times, if needed. When pureed, add one cup of cream and process until creamy. Transfer to a bowl. Repeat the procedure with the remaining scallops, egg yolk, and cream. Combine with the first batch and mix well. Fold in the drained cooked scallops.

Butter a 2-quart mold with 1 tablespoon of butter and fill with the mousse mixture. Cover with a sheet of buttered waxed paper, buttered side down. Place the mousse in a water bath and bake for 45 minutes, or until a knife inserted in the center comes out clean. Prepare the tomato sauce as directed (see following recipe).

Remove the waxed paper and pull off the brown skin on the surface of the mousse. Unmold onto a serving platter. Drain any liquid that accumulates around the base and add to the sauce. Pour the sauce over the mousse and sprinkle with minced parsley.

The mousse can be prepared for baking the night before. The sauce also can be made the night before.

Serves 6.

TOMATO MUSHROOM CREAM SAUCE FOR SCALLOP MOUSSE

3 tablespoons butter	3 tomatoes, peeled, seeded, and
3 tablespoons flour	chopped
poaching liquor from scallops	1 tablespoon butter
1 cup thinly sliced mushrooms	1 cup heavy cream
1 tablespoon butter	salt, pepper, and nutmeg to taste

In a 1-quart saucepan, melt the butter, stir in the flour, and cook the roux until it just starts to turn golden. Stir in the poaching liquor and cook, stirring, until thickened and smooth.

In a small skillet, saute the mushrooms in 1 tablespoon butter until tender. Add mushrooms and their liquid to the sauce.

In the same skillet, saute the tomatoes in remaining butter for 10 minutes. Add to the sauce with the heavy cream. Heat the sauce, stirring. Correct seasoning with salt, pepper, and nutmeg.

Yields about 3 cups.

Shrimp and Scallop Quenelles with Tarragon Sauce

½ pound scallops	2 egg whites
½ pound shrimp, shelled and deveined	dash of cayenne pepper
1 cup heavy cream	salt and pepper to taste

In a processor, puree the scallops and shrimp. With the motor running, slowly add the cream, egg whites, cayenne, and salt and pepper to taste. Process until smooth. Chill for at least two hours, or overnight.

Fit a 14-inch pastry bag with a #8 large plain tip and fill with the quenelles mixture. Fill a large skillet with boiling salted water and put over heat. Keep the water just below the boiling point. Pipe out sections of mixture, about 2 inches long, into the simmering liquid, using a knife to cut them off. Poach for about 5 minutes until they float to the surface. Remove from the liquid with a slotted spoon and drain on paper towels. Set aside.

Prepare sauce (see following recipe). Place cooked quenelles on an ovenproof serving platter, pour on the sauce, and reheat at 350° F.

These can be made the day before and reheated. Can be frozen.

Serves 4 to 6.

TARRAGON SAUCE FOR SHRIMP AND SCALLOP QUENELLES

3 cups heavy cream	salt and pepper to taste
1 tablespoon dried tarragon	

In a 2-quart saucepan, combine the cream and tarragon and simmer until the cream is reduced to 1½ cups. Strain and season with salt and pepper.

Baked Haddock Cottage-Style

3½ pounds haddock fillets	6 mushrooms, minced
salt and pepper to taste	2 tablespoons minced parsley
juice of 1 lemon	½ cup butter, melted
12 Common crackers, crushed	16 thin slices bacon
6 scallions, thinly sliced	

Preheat oven to 400° F.

Sandwich the fish fillets and arrange in a buttered baking pan. Season with salt, pepper, and lemon juice.

In a bowl, combine the crackers, scallions, mushrooms, parsley, and butter. Spread over the fish and lay the bacon slices on top. Bake until cooked, about 30 minutes depending on the thickness of the fish sandwiches. Allow 10 minutes per inch of thickness.

Can be prepared for baking the night before.

Serves 6 to 8.

Fiskepudding (Norwegian Fish Pudding)

The name of this dish unfortunately is no indication of how good it is. The recipe is one of the simplest dishes to prepare and can be served with any of a number of different sauces.

1½ pounds skinned haddock or cod
    fillets
  2 teaspoons salt
  ¼ cup potato flour
  2 cups milk

2 cups heavy cream
freshly grated nutmeg to taste
sauce (see *note*)
parsley or dill sprigs

Preheat oven to 350° F.

Cut the fish into ½-inch cubes. Place half of them in a processor and process until fine, stopping to scrape down the sides of the container once or twice. Add half the salt and potato flour and mix. With the motor running, add half the milk and cream. Season with nutmeg. When smooth, transfer to a large bowl. Repeat the process with the remaining fish, salt, flour, milk, and cream. Mix the two batches together.

Butter an 8-cup loaf pan, charlotte mold, or souffle dish, or 8 1-cup ramekins. Fill with the fish mixture and cover with a sheet of buttered waxed paper, buttered side down. Place in a water bath and bake for 30 to 50 minutes, or until a knife inserted in the center comes out clean. Remove from the water bath and let stand for 10 minutes. Carefully drain off any liquid in the molds, and unmold onto a heated platter. Serve with one of the sauces listed below and garnish with parsley or dill sprigs. Serve hot or cold.

Can be prepared for baking a day ahead. Can also be frozen before baking.

Serves 8 to 12.

Note: You can also use salmon, sole, scallops, or shrimp to prepare this recipe. This fish mold can be served with Bechamel, Hollandaise, Bearnaise, or almost any sauce used in this book. The lobster, shrimp, and scallop sauces in the chapter on souffles would be particularly appropriate, as would a Hollandaise heavily flavored with dill and perhaps tossed with chopped shrimp.

When the mold is served cold, serve freshly made mayonnaise, highly flavored with mustard and or dill, or a fresh cold tomato sauce.

Baked Fresh Mackerel

½ pound bacon, julienne	4 tomatoes, peeled and diced
1 bunch scallions, thinly sliced	4 bay leaves
4 mackerel fillets	minced parsley
salt and pepper to taste	12 littleneck clams
juice of 1 lemon	
1 pound mushrooms, thinly sliced	

Preheat oven to 400° F.

In a small skillet, saute the bacon and scallions until soft, but not brown.

In a baking pan, arrange the fillets in one layer and season with salt, pepper, and lemon juice. Scatter mushrooms, scallion-bacon mixture, tomatoes, bay leaves, and parsley over the fish. Rinse the clams and arrange around the fish. Cover the pan with foil and bake 20 minutes.

Can be prepared for baking the night before.

Serves 4 to 6.

Creamed Poached Salmon with Peas

2 cups cream sauce (see Appendix)	1 cup cooked peas
1 pound poached salmon, flaked	6 slices buttered toast

In a saucepan, heat the cream sauce and gently fold in the salmon and peas. Heat until hot. Arrange buttered toast on serving plates and serve the salmon on top.

The creamed salmon can be prepared the day before and reheated.

Serves 6.

Mousse de Saumon (Salmon Mousse)

1¼ pounds salmon fillets	cayenne pepper to taste
2 large egg whites	1½ cups Hollandaise sauce
1¾ cups heavy cream	2 cups sauteed mushroom caps
1 teaspoon salt	minced parsley

Preheat oven to 350° F.

In a food processor, grind the salmon into a puree. With the machine running, add the egg whites and gradually pour in the cream. Add the salt and cayenne and mix well.

Butter a 1½-quart mold and fill with the salmon mixture. Place in a water bath and bake for 35 to 40 minutes, or until a knife tests clean. Unmold onto a serving platter. Coat with Hollandaise, arrange mushroom caps around the outside edge, and sprinkle with minced parsley.

Can be prepared for baking the night before.

Serves 4 to 6.

Sole and Spinach Casserole with Noodles

6 fillets of sole	nutmeg to taste
2 tablespoons minced shallots	2 egg yolks
salt and pepper to taste	¼ pound fine egg noodles, cooked
½ cup dry white wine	
6 tablespoons butter	1 pound spinach, cooked, drained, and minced
4 tablespoons flour	
2 cups milk	2 tablespoons grated Parmesan cheese
Tabasco sauce to taste	

Preheat oven to 400° F.

Separate the fillets down the center line and fold each in half. Butter a baking dish and place the fillets in one layer on the bottom. Sprinkle with the shallots, salt, pepper, and wine. Cover with a sheet of foil and bake for about 5 minutes. Carefully remove fish to a platter. Reduce the poaching liquor by half.

In a 1-quart saucepan, melt the butter, stir in the flour, and cook the roux until it starts to turn golden. Add the milk, salt, pepper, Tabasco, nutmeg, and fish liquor. Cook, stirring, for 5 minutes, until thickened and smooth. Remove from the heat.

In a small bowl, beat the egg yolks with 4 tablespoons of hot sauce. Return the egg mixture to the sauce. Cook over medium heat until almost boiling but do not boil.

Toss the cooked noodles with 1 tablespoon of butter and season with salt and pepper. Arrange noodles in an ovenproof serving dish. Place the spinach on top of the noodles and arrange the fish on the spinach. Spoon the sauce over the fish and sprinkle with the cheese. Bake about 20 minutes, or until heated through.

Can be prepared for reheating the night before. Reheat at 350° F. until bubbling.

Serves 6.

Espadon en Brochettes (Swordfish on Skewers)

2 pounds swordfish, 1½-inch
   cubes
1 cup olive oil
¼ teaspoon pepper

1 tablespoon minced parsley
salt to taste
1 cucumber, ⅛-inch thick slices
8 tablespoons anchovy butter

Preheat broiler.

Marinate the fish in the olive oil, pepper, parsley, and salt for at least 30 minutes.

Sprinkle the cucumber slices with salt and drain 20 minutes. Rinse cucumbers and pat dry. Arrange the fish and cucumbers alternately on skewers. Broil about 10 to 15 minutes. Serve with anchovy butter on the side.

Can be prepared for broiling the night before. Leave fish in the marinade.

Serves 6.

Curried Shrimp

4 tablespoons butter
1 cup minced onion
1 cup minced carrot
1 cup minced celery
1 cup minced green pepper
1 cup minced green beans
1 cup minced red pepper
salt and cayenne pepper to taste
2 tablespoons curry powder

1 teaspoon nutmeg
½ teaspoon mace
4 tablespoons flour
3 cups sour cream
1 tablespoon paprika
2 pounds shrimp, peeled and
   deveined
3 cups cooked rice

In a 2-quart saucepan, melt the butter and add the vegetables in layers as listed. Season with salt and cayenne. Cover tightly and cook over low heat for 30 minutes. Stir and cook 10 minutes longer.

Remove from the heat and stir in the curry powder, nutmeg, mace, and flour. Stir in the sour cream and paprika and heat gently without boiling. Stir in the shrimp and let cook gently until shrimp are cooked, about 5 minutes or less depending on the size of the shrimp. Do not overcook. Serve with rice.

Can be prepared the day before and reheated in a casserole at 350° F. Can be frozen and reheated.

Serves 6.

Shrimp Bel Paese

2 pounds shrimp, peeled and deveined
1 cup clam juice
3 slices lemon
¼ teaspoon crushed garlic
6 thin slices onion
⅔ cup dry sherry
1 cup grated Bel Paese cheese

Preheat broiler.

In a 1-quart casserole, combine the shrimp, clam juice, water to cover, lemon slices, garlic, and onion. Bring to a boil and drain, discarding garlic and onion. Place shrimp in a casserole and pour on the sherry. Sprinkle with the cheese. Broil until cheese is melted and golden. Serve at once.

Can be prepared for broiling the night before.

Serves 4 to 6.

Shrimp and Corn Casserole

1½ pounds shrimp, peeled and deveined
3 tablespoons butter
½ teaspoon salt
pepper to taste
cayenne pepper to taste
¼ cup minced onion
2½ cups corn, drained
8 stuffed olives, sliced
1 cup heavy cream
minced parsley

In a 10-inch skillet, saute the shrimp in the butter until they start to turn pink. Season with salt, pepper, and cayenne. Add the onion and simmer 1 minute longer. Stir in the corn, olives, and cream. Heat. Serve sprinkled with the parsley.

Do not prepare ahead.

Serves 6 to 8.

CHAPTER 8
Chicken and Meat

Probably the meat most associated with breakfast and brunch is bacon, closely followed by sausage and ham. All of these are very good indeed, but there are many chicken and meat dishes that can be served as well.

Broiled meat is very palatable at this hour, whether it is a substantial steak, kidneys, liver, or lamb chops. Stews are particularly welcome in the winter months for their full warming flavors, and they are easier on the host-cook. In general, the most popular meat dishes for breakfast and brunch can be prepared ahead and often frozen.

Chicken, Broccoli, and Noodle Casserole

3 cups poached, diced chicken
4 cups Sauce Supreme (see Appendix)
1 bunch broccoli, broken into florets and cooked
salt, pepper, and nutmeg to taste

¼ pound fine or medium noodles, cooked
4 tablespoons butter
¼ cup grated Gruyere or Parmesan cheese

Preheat oven to 350° F.

In a large bowl, combine the chicken, 2 cups sauce, and broccoli. Season with salt, pepper, and nutmeg to taste. Toss the noodles with the butter and arrange in a buttered, ovenproof serving dish. Arrange chicken mixture on top and pour on the remaining sauce. Sprinkle with the cheese and bake until bubbling hot.

Can be prepared for baking and frozen.

Serves 6.

Chicken Saute Washington

2½ pound chicken, cut up
salt and pepper to taste
2 tablespoons butter
1 tablespoon minced shallot

2 tablespoons bourbon
2 cups heavy cream
10 ounces cooked corn

Sprinkle the chicken pieces with salt and pepper. In a 10-inch skillet, saute the chicken until golden and cooked through. Remove chicken to a serving platter.

Pour off the excess fat from the skillet and add the butter and shallots. Cook until soft. Add the whiskey and deglaze the pan. Stir in the cream, salt, and pepper. Simmer until the sauce is reduced to 1 cup. Add the corn and heat. Pour over the chicken and serve.

Can be prepared the day before and reheated.

Serves 4.

Chicken with Lemon Cream

3½ pound chicken, split in half
2 tablespoons butter
4 thin slices lemon
2 tablespoons dry sherry

½ cup heavy cream
4 thin slices Gruyere cheese
salt and pepper to taste

Preheat the oven to 350° F.

Place the chicken, skin side up, in a shallow baking pan. Dot with butter and bake in the upper third of the oven for 30 minutes. Place a slice of lemon on each leg and breast of the chicken. Combine the sherry and cream, pour over the chicken, and bake another 30 minutes.

Remove the lemon slices and place cheese slices on top of the chicken. Bake until melted. Remove chicken to a serving platter and season pan juices with salt and pepper. Pour over the chicken and serve. Best served immediately.

Serves 4.

Creamed Chicken Chestershire

3 cups cooked, diced chicken
1 cup light cream
2 cups Bechamel sauce

4 English muffins, split and toasted
8 thin slices cheddar cheese
paprika

Preheat broiler.

In a 1½-quart saucepan, gently simmer the chicken and cream for 10 minutes. Stir in the Bechamel. Arrange the muffins on an ovenproof serving platter and cover with the chicken mixture. Place a slice of cheese on each and dust with paprika. Glaze under the broiler.

Do not assemble more than a few minutes before broiling.

Serves 4 to 8.

Chicken Livers in Red Wine

½ pound mushroom caps	½ cup red wine
2 green peppers, minced	1 bay leaf
3 tablespoons butter	salt and pepper to taste
1½ pounds chicken livers	hot buttered toast
4 tablespoons butter	

In a 10-inch skillet, saute the mushrooms and peppers in 3 tablespoons butter until soft.

In a separate skillet, saute the chicken livers in the remaining butter until browned, but still pink inside. Add to the mushroom mixture with the wine, bay leaf, salt, and pepper. Simmer 10 minutes. Serve on toast.

Can be prepared the day before and reheated. Can also be frozen and reheated.

Serves 6.

Chicken Livers and Grapes

1½ pounds chicken livers	3 cups cooked brown rice
4 tablespoons butter	½ cup port
½ pound green, seedless grapes	small bunch of grapes

In a 12-inch skillet, saute the livers in the butter until browned, but still rare. Add the grapes and heat. With a slotted spoon, remove the livers and grapes to a serving platter. Surround with the rice. Add the port to the skillet and reduce by half over high heat. Pour over livers and garnish with a small bunch of grapes.

Serves 4 to 6.

Beef Stroganoff

1 pound lean beef fillet, in ¼-inch strips	½ cup beef stock
1 tablespoon paprika	1 cup sour cream
3 tablespoons vegetable oil	1 teaspoon lemon juice
¼ pound mushrooms, thinly sliced	salt to taste
¼ cup dry sherry	½ pound fine noodles, cooked

Sprinkle the beef strips with paprika. In a large skillet, saute the beef in the oil until browned, but still rare. Do not crowd the pan. Remove the meat from the pan. Add the mushrooms and saute until tender. Remove the mushrooms.

Add the sherry to the pan and reduce by half. Add the beef stock and simmer 5 minutes. Remove from the heat and stir in the sour cream, lemon juice, and salt. Add the mushrooms and meat and reheat, but do not boil. Serve over the noodles.

Can be prepared ahead and reheated gently.

Serves 6.

Boeuf en Casserole Provencale
(Braised Beef Provencale)

2½ pounds eye round	2 teaspoons potato flour
3 tablespoons butter	1 teaspoon meat glaze
2 tablespoons cognac	½ cup hearty red wine
3 onions, cut in eighths	1 cup chicken stock
½ teaspoon minced garlic	¼ cup dry sherry
4 large tomatoes, peeled and chopped	1 teaspoon currant jelly
½ cup stuffed olives	1 bay leaf
2 teaspoons tomato paste	2 tablespoons minced parsley

Cut the beef into 1½-inch cubes. In a large skillet, saute the meat in 2 tablespoons butter until browned. Remove meat from the pan and set aside. Add the cognac to the pan, ignite, and cook, stirring up the browned bits. Add remaining butter, onion, and garlic to the pan and saute briskly for 5 minutes, or until lightly glazed. Add tomatoes and olives and cook for 2 minutes. Remove from heat.

In a small bowl, combine the tomato paste, flour, and meat glaze. Stir into the pan, and add the wine, chicken stock, and sherry. Return the pan to the heat and cook, stirring, until the sauce comes to a boil. Add the beef, jelly, and bay leaf. Cover and simmer over low heat for 45 to 60 minutes, or until very tender. Serve garnished with parsley.

Can be made ahead and reheated. Can be frozen.

Serves 6.

Mexican Beef with Orange

2 cloves garlic	½ cup water
1 teaspoon ground coriander	1 onion
½ teaspoon ground cloves	1 bay leaf
¾ teaspoon salt	1 quart orange juice
¼ teaspoon pepper	3 oranges, thinly sliced
3 pounds beef round	

In a mortar and pestle, or a blender, grind the garlic, coriander, cloves, salt, and pepper into a paste. With a small knife, make slits in the roast and fill with the garlic mixture. Place the meat in a casserole and add the water, onion, and bay leaf. Simmer until tender, about 2½ hours. Cool.

Slice the meat, arrange on a platter, and pour on the orange juice. Marinate overnight. Garnish with orange slices.

Must be prepared ahead. Can be frozen.

Serves 6.

Beef and Sausage with Curried Noodles

4 tablespoons butter	¾ cup chopped onion
2 pounds beef round, in 1-inch cubes	¼ cup butter
4 cups water	6 tablespoons flour
2 bay leaves	½ cup heavy cream
1 teaspoon salt	8 ounces egg noodles
1 pound kielbasa, thinly sliced	½ teaspoon curry powder
1 cup sliced celery	½ pound snow peas, blanched

In a large skillet, heat 4 tablespoons butter and brown the beef. Add the water, bay leaves, and salt. Simmer gently until tender, about 1 hour. Drain the meat and reserve 3 cups of liquid.

Broil the sausage until browned.

In a 2-quart saucepan, saute the celery and onion in the ¼ cup butter until soft. Add the flour and cook, stirring, until it begins to turn golden. Stir in the beef broth and the cream. Cook, stirring, until thickened and smooth. Add the sausage and beef. Reheat.

In 3 quarts of boiling water, cook the egg noodles and the curry powder. Drain the noodles and arrange on a serving platter. Add the snow peas to the beef mixture and serve over the noodles.

Can be reheated. Can be assembled with noodles in an ovenproof serving dish, frozen, and reheated at 350° F. in the dish.

Serves 6.

Creamed Chipped Beef on Toast

¼ pound chipped beef	1 cup heavy cream
4 tablespoons butter	salt and pepper to taste
3 tablespoons flour	buttered toast points
1 cup milk	

If the beef is very salty, run under cold water for 30 seconds and drain. Cut beef into shreds. In a 9-inch skillet, heat the beef in the butter until the edges start to curl. Sprinkle with the flour and cook 1 minute, stirring often. Stir in the milk and cream and cook, stirring, until the mixture thickens. Correct seasoning with salt and pepper. Serve on buttered toast points.

Can be prepared ahead and reheated. Can be frozen.

Serves 4.

Note: There are several versions of this dish, this being the simplest. You can add ½ pound thinly sliced mushrooms sauteed in 2 tablespoons butter, if desired. Or stir in 2 ounces sliced pimientos or 2 cups of grated cheddar. Or you can add all of these ingredients together.

Meat Loaf in Sour Cream Pastry

1 recipe sour cream pastry (see Appendix)	¼ cup minced parsley
	1 cup grated Emmenthal cheese
¾ cup minced mushrooms	½ cup milk
4 tablespoons butter	1 egg
3 pounds ground meat (beef, pork, or veal, or a combination)	2 tablespoons milk
	2 cups sour cream
½ cup minced onions	

Prepare pastry and chill 1 hour.

Preheat oven to 375° F.

In a large skillet, saute the mushrooms in the butter until lightly colored. Add the meat and cook, stirring, for 8 to 10 minutes, or until it loses its color and any liquid has evaporated. Scrape into a large bowl and stir in the onions, parsley, cheese, and milk. Mix well.

Divide the dough in half and roll one half into a 6 by 14 inch rectangle. Place on a buttered baking sheet. Place the meat mixture in a mound in the center of the pastry. Roll remaining pastry into a 6 by 14 inch rectangle and place over the meat. Press the edges of the pastry together. Combine the egg and milk and brush over the pastry. Cut a hole to let the steam escape. Use any remaining pastry to make strips or designs on top of the loaf. Brush once again with egg-milk mixture. Bake for 45 minutes. Serve with sour cream.

Can be prepared for baking the day before, or frozen.

Serves 6.

Tendrons de Veau a l'Estragon (Breast of Veal with Tarragon)

2 pounds boned breast of veal	½ cup water
6 tablespoons clarified butter	2 teaspoons dried tarragon
3 tablespoons flour	salt and pepper to taste
½ cup white wine	

Preheat the oven to 300° F.

Cut the veal into 1 by 3 inch strips. In a large skillet, saute the veal in the butter until golden. Sprinkle with flour and cook until the flour is golden. Stir in the wine and water and cook, stirring, until the sauce has thickened.

Transfer to a flame-proof casserole and bring to a boil on top of the stove. Season with salt, pepper, and 1 teaspoon tarragon. Bake 1½ hours. Ten minutes before the cooking period ends, add remaining tarragon.

Can be prepared ahead and reheated, or frozen.

Serves 4.

Veal and Sausage Ragout

3 onions, thinly sliced	2 tomatoes, quartered
2 tablespoons butter	1 green pepper, sliced
1 pound veal shoulder, in ¾-inch cubes	½ pound kielbasa, thinly sliced
2 tablespoons paprika	1 cup sour cream

In a large skillet, saute the onions in the butter until soft, but not brown. Add the veal and paprika and saute for 10 minutes. Add the tomatoes, pepper, and sausage and simmer until tender, about 35 minutes. Remove the pan from the heat and, without boiling, stir in the sour cream.

Can be prepared ahead and reheated, or frozen.

Serves 4 to 6.

Roghan Josh (Curried Lamb)

2 pounds lamb, in 1 by 2 inch pieces
½ teaspoon cayenne pepper
1 teaspoon salt
1 cup plain yogurt
1 tablespoon minced gingerroot
¼ cup clarified butter
pepper to taste

½ teaspoon turmeric
2 tablespoons minced fresh coriander
1 cup water
½ teaspoon garam masala (see note)
pinch of ground nutmeg

In a 2-quart bowl, combine the lamb, cayenne, and salt and mix well. Add the yogurt and ginger and mix well. Cover and marinate at room temperature for 1 hour.

In a skillet, heat the butter until hot and stir in the pepper and turmeric. Add the lamb and its marinade and heat, stirring meat constantly, until it comes to a boil. Lower heat and simmer uncovered 1 hour.

Sprinkle mixture with coriander and pour ½ cup water down one side of the pan. Cover and simmer 15 minutes. Stir in ¼ cup of water, cover, and simmer 15 minutes. Stir in remaining water and cook 10 more minutes. Pour meat into a serving bowl and sprinkle with garam masala and nutmeg.

Can be prepared ahead and reheated, or frozen.

Serves 4 to 6.

Note: Garam masala is a mixture of spices available in oriental markets.

Ham Hash

3 tablespoons butter
2 cups finely chopped ham
2 cups sliced cooked potato

1 cup sour cream
salt and pepper to taste
2 tablespoons minced chives

In a 10-inch skillet, melt the butter, add the ham and potatoes, and heat. Stir in the sour cream and season with salt and pepper. Heat but do not boil. Serve sprinkled with chives.

Should be prepared just before serving.

Serves 4 to 6.

Sausages a la Campagnarde

3 tomatoes, chopped
salt and pepper to taste
1/4 cup olive oil
6 Italian sweet sausages
2 tablespoons dry white wine
1 large onion, thinly sliced
1 teaspoon minced garlic
1/2 pound mushrooms, thinly sliced
2 green peppers, peeled and sliced

1/2 teaspoon paprika
1/4 teaspoon hot pepper
1/4 teaspoon dried thyme
1/4 teaspoon dried rosemary
1/2 cup diced pimiento
2 tablespoons minced garlic
2 tablespoons minced parsley

Place tomatoes in a colander. Sprinkle with salt and let drain for 30 minutes.

In a 9-inch skillet, heat 2 tablespoons of oil and add the sausages and wine. Cook over low heat until browned. Remove to a plate and discard the fat.

Add the remaining oil to a large skillet and saute the onion and 1 teaspoon garlic until soft, but not brown. Add the mushrooms, peppers, and salt and pepper to taste. Cook 4 minutes. Stir in the paprika, hot pepper, thyme, rosemary, and tomatoes. Add the sausages and cook over medium heat until tomato juices have evaporated. Correct seasoning. Arrange on a serving platter and sprinkle with pimiento, garlic, and parsley.

Can be prepared ahead and reheated, or frozen.

Serves 4 to 6.

Sausages and Apples

1 pound pork sausage links
1 cup maple syrup
1/2 cup white vinegar

4 medium apples, cored, in 1/2-inch slices

In a 9-inch skillet, saute the sausages until brown. Drain.

In a 1-quart saucepan, bring the maple syrup and vinegar to a boil. Add the apples and simmer until tender crisp. Drain. Arrange sausages on a platter and surround with apples.

Can be prepared the night before and reheated.

Serves 4.

CHAPTER 9
Vegetables

Potatoes are the most popular breakfast vegetable. Usually temperate eaters will scoop up an extra serving of hashed brown potatoes without a second thought; the most stringent waist watcher will down a second helping of potato pancakes.

Other vegetables, however, are not as popular. Often, broiled tomatoes are not only a second choice but the final one. There are, however, many delicious vegetable preparations that can serve not only as a side dish but also often as a main course.

Asparagus Pie

2 cups heavy cream	3 tablespoons minced lean ham
1 large bay leaf	1 tablespoon butter
4 sprigs parsley	1 9-inch pie shell, fully baked
4 thin slices onion	1 pound asparagus, cooked
pinch of thyme	½ cup grated Gruyere cheese
pinch of marjoram	¾ cup fresh bread crumbs
6 whole peppercorns	butter

Preheat broiler.

In a 1½-quart saucepan, simmer the cream, bay leaf, parsley, onion, thyme, marjoram, and peppercorns for 15 minutes. Strain.

In a 1-quart saucepan, heat the ham in the butter and add the cream. Reduce to 1 cup. Line the pie shell with asparagus spears. Pour on just enough sauce to cover the asparagus. Stir the cheese into the remaining sauce and pour on top. Sprinkle with bread crumbs and dot generously with butter. Glaze under the broiler.

Do not assemble and glaze until shortly before serving. You can substitute fennel, spinach, broccoli, or snow peas for the asparagus.

Serves 6.

Carrot Tart

2 pounds carrots, sliced
½ teaspoon sugar
½ teaspoon salt
⅓ cup butter

pepper to taste
⅛ teaspoon lemon juice
1 9-inch pie shell, fully baked
3 scallions, minced

Preheat oven to 350° F.

In a 2-quart saucepan, add enough water to cover the carrots. Add the sugar and salt and simmer until the water has been absorbed and the carrots are tender. If added texture is desired, set aside 1½ cups carrots. Otherwise, add butter to the carrots and force through a food mill or ricer, or puree in a processor. Season the pureed carrots with pepper and lemon juice.

Spread the carrot puree in the bottom of the pie shell. (Arrange any reserved carrot slices in concentric circles on the top.) Sprinkle with scallions. Reheat in the oven for about 20 minutes.

The carrots can be cooked the day before and the prebaked shell can be frozen. Do not assemble until shortly before serving. This tart can also be made with parsnips or turnips.

Baked Eggplant with Cheese

3 medium eggplants, peeled and
   cubed
salt
water
½ cup minced onion
4 eggs
½ cup grated Parmesan cheese

¼ cup heavy cream
4 tablespoons butter
4 tomatoes, peeled and thinly sliced
2 tablespoons minced fresh basil
1 cup buttered bread crumbs
½ cup grated Gruyere or Parmesan
   cheese

Preheat oven to 350° F.

Sprinkle the eggplant cubes generously with salt and place in a colander. Drain for 30 minutes. Meanwhile, in a large kettle, bring 3 quarts of water to boil with 2 teaspoons of salt and the onion. Add the eggplant and simmer 10 minutes. Drain well.

In a medium bowl, combine the eggs, ½ cup Parmesan, and cream. Mix well.

Butter a 2-quart casserole or souffle dish. Arrange a layer of eggplant cubes in the bottom of the casserole, place some tomato slices on top, and sprinkle with basil. Continue to layer the vegetables and basil, ending with a layer of tomatoes. Pour the egg mixture over the top and let it run down through the vegetable layers. Sprinkle the top with bread crumbs and the remaining cheese. Bake 45 minutes.

Can be prepared for baking the day before and reheated. Can be frozen. Serves 6 to 8.

Leek and Mushroom Tart

1½ pounds leeks, trimmed, washed, and thinly sliced
8 tablespoons butter
⅔ cup heavy cream
salt and pepper to taste

½ pound mushrooms, thinly sliced
pastry for 1 2-crust, 9-inch pie
1 egg yolk
1 teaspoon water

Preheat oven to 400° F.

In a 1½-quart saucepan, saute the leeks in 5 tablespoons butter, stirring, for 4 minutes. Add ¼ cup water, cover the pan, and simmer, stirring occasionally, for 15 to 20 minutes or until tender. Uncover the pan and cook over high heat, stirring, until the liquid has evaporated. Set aside.

In a 3-cup saucepan, simmer the cream until it is reduced by half. Stir the cream into the cooked leeks and season with salt and pepper. In a 9-inch skillet, saute the mushrooms in the remaining butter until lightly browned.

Roll half of the pastry to line the bottom of a 9-inch pie tin, a tart pan with a removable bottom, or a quiche dish. Fill the pie shell with the leeks and top with mushrooms. Roll the remaining pastry to form a top for the tart. Crimp top and bottom edges together. Cut a hole in the top to allow steam to escape.

In a small bowl, combine the egg yolk and water and brush over the surface of the tart. With the point of a small sharp knife, score the surface, making shallow decorative lines across the surface of the pastry without cutting through it. Bake for 15 minutes. Lower the heat to 350° F. and bake another 35 to 40 minutes, or until it is golden brown and crisp. Let stand 20 minutes before serving. Serve warm.

Can be prepared for baking the day before, or frozen. Can also be frozen after baking. You can substitute grated, drained zucchini, celery, fennel, or onions for the leeks.

Serves 6 to 8.

Sauteed Mushrooms

2 pounds mushrooms   1 tablespoon lemon juice
8 tablespoons butter   salt and pepper to taste

The mushrooms can be cut into slices, quarters, or halves. If small, leave them whole.

In a 12-inch skillet, melt the butter until very hot, but not burned. Add the mushrooms and cook, stirring constantly, for 2 minutes. Add the lemon juice and continue cooking until the mushrooms are tender. Season with salt and pepper.

Can be prepared ahead and reheated. Can be frozen.

Serves 6 to 8.

Deep-Fried Mushrooms

1 pound of fresh button mushrooms   salt and pepper to taste
½ cup flour   2 cups fresh bread crumbs, no
2 eggs   crusts
¼ cup water   ¼ teaspoon dried thyme
1 tablespoon olive oil   oil for deep frying (see *note*)

Rinse the mushrooms in a colander, drain well, and dredge in the flour. In a medium bowl, beat together the eggs, water, olive oil, salt, and pepper. In another bowl, combine the bread crumbs and thyme.

Heat the oil to 360° F. in a saucepan. Dip the mushrooms in the egg mixture, then roll in the bread crumbs. Fry until golden and drain on paper toweling. Serve immediately.

The mushrooms can be prepared for frying the night before and kept on a cake rack in the refrigerator. They must be served immediately after frying.

Yields about 24.

Note: Do not fill the saucepan more than half full of oil.

Zweibeltort (Onion Pie)

6 large Spanish onions   1 cup milk
6 tablespoons butter   ½ cup grated Gruyere or Muenster
salt and pepper to taste   cheese
2 eggs, lightly beaten

Preheat oven to 350° F.

The success of this dish depends on the quantity of onions and the slow cooking. Use at least 3 pounds of thinly, almost transparently, sliced onions and cook them at least 45 minutes before finishing the tart.

In a 12-inch skillet, melt the butter over low heat. Add the onions, cover, and cook, stirring occasionally, for 35 minutes over very low heat. Remove the cover and cook, stirring, over low heat until the onions start to turn golden and are almost a puree. The onions should be golden; they must not brown. Season with salt and pepper. Remove from the heat and cool 10 minutes.

Lightly butter a 10-inch quiche dish or cake pan. In a small bowl, combine the eggs and milk and stir into the onion mixture. Pour into the prepared baking dish and sprinkle with cheese. Bake 25 to 30 minutes or until set.

Can be prepared for baking the day before. Onions can be frozen.

Serves 6 to 8.

Epinards Gratinees (Spinach Gratin)

2 pounds spinach, cooked and chopped	3 cups Mornay sauce
salt, pepper, and nutmeg to taste	½ cup grated Gruyere or Parmesan cheese
4 tablespoons butter	

Preheat oven to 350° F.

Squeeze the spinach dry, place in a bowl, and season with salt, pepper, and nutmeg. Stir in 3 tablespoons of butter, and 1½ cups Mornay sauce. Butter an 8 by 11 baking dish with remaining butter and put spinach in the dish. Coat the top with remaining sauce and sprinkle with cheese. Bake until bubbling hot and lightly browned.

Can be prepared for baking the day before. Can be frozen before baking.

Serves 6 to 8.

Note: Although we have suggested spinach for this preparation, almost any vegetable can be treated in the same manner. For example, you can use asparagus, artichoke hearts, carrots, cauliflower, broccoli, beans, celery, fennel, mushrooms, potatoes, or zucchini. Although Mornay sauce is made with Gruyere or Parmesan, you can be as inventive, within reason, as you choose. Try using feta or one of the many chevres for a flavor change, or use Italian fontina. Try combining a milk cheese, such as farmer, with a strong-flavored cheese, such as Stilton, Gorgonzola, or Roquefort.

Baked Zucchini

6 small zucchini   ½ cup buttered bread crumbs
2 tablespoons minced shallots   salt and pepper to taste

Preheat the oven to 350° F.

Cut the zucchini in half lengthwise. With a small sharp knife, make cross hatch cuts in the cut surface of the zucchini. Sprinkle with salt and let drain for 20 minutes. If the salt has not drained off, run under cold water. Arrange the zucchini in one layer in a baking dish, and add ¼ inch of boiling water. Sprinkle the shallots and bread crumbs over the zucchini and season with salt and pepper to taste. Bake, uncovered, until tender and lightly browned, about 30 minutes.

Can be prepared for baking the night before.

Serves 6.

Hashed Brown Potatoes (Dit Pommes a la Lyonnaise)

1 medium onion, chopped   salt and pepper to taste
6 tablespoons butter   1 tablespoon minced parsley
3 cups cold, sliced, boiled potatoes

In a 10-inch skillet, saute the onions in the butter until soft, but not brown. Add the potatoes and cook, stirring occasionally, over medium heat until browned on the edges. Season with salt and pepper. Serve sprinkled with minced parsley.

These should be cooked slowly. Once prepared, they can be reheated.

Serves 6.

Roesti (Swiss-Style Fried Potato Cake)

3 pounds baking potatoes, peeled   salt and pepper to taste
8 tablespoons butter

Just before cooking, grate the potatoes and rinse under cold running water. Drain and dry with paper toweling.

In a 9-inch skillet, melt 4 tablespoons of butter and add the potatoes. Press potatoes into a flat cake. Cook over medium heat for about 15 minutes. Check to make sure potatoes are not burning. Season with salt and pepper.

With a spatula, loosen the cake and slide it onto a dinner plate. Add remaining butter to the pan and flip the potato cake into the pan. Season the top with salt and pepper. Cook until golden on the second side. Cut into wedges and serve at once.

Cannot be made ahead.

Serves 6 to 8.

Potato Pancakes

6 medium potatoes, peeled	3 tablespoons flour
1 small onion, grated	1/4 teaspoon baking powder
2 eggs, lightly beaten	vegetable oil
1 teaspoon salt	apple sauce or sour cream
pepper to taste	

Just before making the pancakes, grate the potatoes and combine with the onion, eggs, salt, pepper, flour, and baking powder. Mix well. Pour off any accumulated liquid and use the mixture immediately. (It will turn dark if allowed to stand for more than a few minutes.)

In a 10-inch skillet, heat 1/4 inch of oil. Drop the batter by spoonfuls to make pancakes about 2 1/2 inches wide. Fry until golden on one side, turn, and fry the other side. Drain on paper toweling for a few minutes and serve. Serve apple sauce or sour cream on the side.

Serves 6.

Note: If necessary, you can keep potato pancakes warm on a baking sheet lined with paper toweling in a 250° F. oven. They can be frozen and reheated in the oven, if desired. They are at their best when freshly prepared and served immediately.

Potato Almond Croquettes

3 cups hot mashed potatoes	1 egg
3 tablespoons butter	2 tablespoons water
3/4 teaspoon salt, or to taste	1/2 cup sliced almonds
2 egg yolks	oil for deep frying

In a medium bowl, beat together the potatoes, butter, salt, and egg yolks. Shape the mixture into 6 to 12 croquettes, depending on the desired size. They can be shaped like balls, pyramids, or wine corks.

In a small bowl, beat the egg with the water. Roll the croquettes in the egg mixture, then in the almonds, and again in the egg mixture.

In a saucepan, heat the oil to 360° F. Deep fry the croquettes until golden and drain on paper toweling.

Serves 6.

Note: Can be prepared for deep frying the night before. Can be frozen after frying and reheated at 350° F. on a cake rack lined with paper towels. They are best when freshly fried and served immediately.

Jansson's Frestelse (Jansson's Temptation)

4 baking potatoes, peeled	pepper to taste
2½ tablespoons butter	2 tablespoons bread crumbs
2 tablespoons vegetable oil	2 tablespoons butter
2 large onions, thinly sliced	1 cup heavy cream
18 anchovy fillets	½ cup milk

Preheat the oven to 400° F.

Cut the potatoes into julienne strips, ¼ inch thick and 2 inches long. Hold in a bowl of cold water to prevent discoloring.

In a large skillet, heat 2 tablespoons of butter and the oil. Cook the onions in the skillet until soft, but not brown.

Butter a 1½- to 2-quart baking dish with ½ tablespoon butter. Drain potatoes and pat dry. Arrange a layer of potatoes in the dish, then a layer of onions and a layer of anchovies. Continue layering, ending with potatoes. Sprinkle each layer with a little pepper. Sprinkle the bread crumbs over the top and dot with remaining butter.

In a small saucepan, heat the cream and milk until almost boiling. Pour over the potatoes and bake for 45 minutes, or until tender. Most of the liquid should be absorbed.

Should be baked and served.

Serves 6.

Rice Fritters

4 large eggs	4 teaspoons sugar
6 tablespoons heavy cream	pinch of salt
2 cups cooked rice	1 cup bread crumbs
2 tablespoons butter	oil for deep frying

In a 1-quart saucepan, beat 2 eggs until frothy. Add 4 tablespoons of cream and the rice. Cook over low heat, stirring constantly, until thickened. Stir in the butter, sugar, and salt. Cool.

Combine the remaining eggs and cream in a small bowl. Place bread crumbs in another bowl. Form the rice mixture into small balls or flat cakes. Dip into the egg mixture and roll in bread crumbs.

Heat the oil in a saucepan to 375° F. Fry croquettes until golden. Drain on paper toweling and serve with honey, maple syrup, or jam of your choice.

Croquettes can be prepared for frying the night before. Can be frozen after frying.

Serves 6.

CHAPTER 10
Pancakes, Doughnuts, Muffins, and Quick Breads

No breakfast or brunch seems complete without some type of bread, whether as a main course, like pancakes, or an accompaniment, like muffins or doughnuts.

The breads in this chapter are made without yeast. They are generally called quick breads because there is no need for them to rise for extended periods of time.

These breads are at their absolute best only minutes from the oven. In fact, they start to lose quality within a few hours. They can be frozen (put them into freezer bags and freeze them as soon as they reach room temperature). However, with a little careful planning you should be able to serve freshly made quick breads, except to large crowds. Assemble the ingredients the night before, measure them, and line them up on a counter in the order needed. Prepare the baking pans also. The next morning, the bread can be prepared and in the oven before the coffee is ready.

PANCAKES

Basic Recipe

2 cups flour	2 eggs
2 teaspoons baking powder	1½ cups sour milk (see *note*) or
1 teaspoon salt	buttermilk
3 tablespoons sugar	2 tablespoons melted butter

In a 1-quart bowl, mix the flour, baking powder, salt, and sugar.

In a small bowl, beat the eggs and milk together and stir into the dry ingredients. Add the melted butter. Let stand 5 minutes.

Heat a griddle, brush with melted butter, and ladle out the batter. Cook until the bubbles on the top have opened and the underside is browned. Turn and cook until golden. Serve hot with creamed, softened butter and a sweet coating of your choice.

Serves 4 to 6.

Note: Do not make the batter more than an hour or so before baking or the baking powder will lose potency. Add more milk if you desire thinner pancakes. For sweet toppings, serve honey, maple syrup, cinnamon sugar, strawberry sauce, blueberry sauce, and the like.

Note: To sour milk, add a few drops of lemon juice or vinegar to sweet milk. It will sour immediately.

Pancake Variations

BLUEBERRY PANCAKES   Toss 1 cup blueberries with ½ cup flour. Stir into the batter just before frying.

APPLE PANCAKES   Saute 2 peeled, sliced apples in 1 tablespoon butter until tender. Sprinkle with sugar, cinnamon, and nutmeg to taste. Ladle the pancake batter onto the griddle and put a tablespoon or more of apple mixture in the center of each pancake before it sets.

CHERRY PANCAKES   Pit 1 cup fresh cherries and add sugar to taste. Add to pancakes in the same manner as apples.

PEACH, NECTARINE, OR APRICOT PANCAKES   Follow directions for apple pancakes.

STRAWBERRY PANCAKES   Follow directions for cherry pancakes, substituting strawberries.

CORNMEAL PANCAKES   Substitute 1 cup cornmeal for 1 cup flour.

Funnel Cakes

2 cups flour	2 eggs, lightly beaten
1 tablespoon sugar	1¼ cups milk
1 teaspoon baking powder	oil for deep frying
¼ teaspoon salt	

In a medium bowl, combine the flour, sugar, baking powder, and salt and mix well. Make a well in the center of the flour and stir in the eggs and milk to form a smooth batter.

In a 12-inch skillet, heat 1½ inches oil until very hot, but not smoking. To shape the cakes, use a funnel with a half-inch opening. Place an index finger under the tip of the funnel and pour in ½ cup of batter. Hold the funnel over the hot fat and rotate it to form spiraling, interconnecting 6 inch rings. Make 2 or 3 cakes at a time. Fry until golden, turn, and fry the other side.

Keep warm on a paper towel lined baking sheet at 250° F. while cooking the remaining batter. If the batter becomes too firm, add more milk, 1 tablespoon at a time. Serve warm cakes with molasses or maple syrup.

Does not keep.

Yields about 12 cakes.

Waffles

1½ cups flour	2 eggs, separated
1 teaspoon baking powder	1 cup sour cream
½ teaspoon salt	2 tablespoons melted butter
½ teaspoon soda	

In a 1-quart bowl, combine the flour, baking powder, salt, and soda and mix well.

In a small bowl, beat the egg yolks with the sour cream and stir into the dry ingredients until well mixed. Stir in the butter. Beat the egg whites until stiff, but not dry. Fold into the batter and cook in the waffle iron according to the manufacturer's directions.

Serves 6.

Note: Serve with the toppings suggested for pancakes or with vanilla ice cream.

Pain Perdu (Lost Bread or French Toast)

6 double-thick slices bread	¾ teaspoon orange liqueur
6 eggs, lightly beaten	butter for frying
¾ cup milk	maple syrup
1 tablespoon sugar	orange butter (see below)
1½ teaspoons rum	

Cut day-old, homemade, French or Italian bread into slices 1½ to 2 inches thick and place in one layer in a baking dish.

In a medium bowl, beat the eggs, milk, sugar, rum, and orange liqueur. Pour over the bread and let stand for at least 10 minutes and up to 12 hours. The longer the bread sits in the liquid, the more it will absorb. However, the slices will also be more difficult to move.

In a skillet, heat the butter. With a spatula, place the bread slices in the pan and saute until golden brown. Turn and cook the second side. Serve at once.

Serves 6.

Note: These puff up as they cook and start to deflate when removed from the heat. Serve with melted butter and any of the toppings suggested for pancakes, or with orange butter.

ORANGE BUTTER   Whip ½ pound unsalted butter with 3 tablespoons sugar until fluffy. Beat in 2 tablespoons grated orange rind and 2 tablespoons orange juice.

DOUGHNUTS

There are two types of doughnuts, those made quickly with baking powder and those made with yeast that take several hours to rise before cooking. This chapter includes both types, even though yeast doughs are considered in the next chapter. Doughnuts are at their best served within minutes of frying. If you must make them ahead, freeze as quickly as possible after frying and reheat at 350° F. before serving.

Doughnuts require gentle handling. If you are rough with the dough, it will be very tough when cooked.

Plain Doughnuts

4 cups flour	2 eggs
1 cup sugar	1 egg yolk
1 tablespoon baking powder	1 cup milk
½ teaspoon ground cinnamon	¼ cup melted butter
½ teaspoon salt	oil for deep frying

Preheat the fat in a large skillet to 375° F.

In a bowl, combine the flour, sugar, baking powder, cinnamon, and salt.

In a small bowl, beat the eggs, egg yolk, and milk until well mixed. Gently stir the liquid ingredients into the dry, along with the melted butter. Mix until just soft enough to handle. Turn onto a well-floured board and press into a flat cake. Roll gently to about a 1 inch thickness. Cut out with a floured doughnut cutter. Cut scraps into 1 inch balls. (It is best not to reroll the dough. Cook the small pieces separately.)

Fry doughnuts until golden on both sides. Drain on paper toweling. Once fried, the doughnuts should be served or frozen.

Plain doughnuts can be rolled in granulated sugar or cinnamon sugar, frosted, or dipped in a thin coating of confectioners' sugar and water, if desired. (See page 166.)

Yields about 18 doughnuts.

Note: The dough will be very soft and can be patted into shape without using a rolling pin.

CRULLERS   Cut the dough, which should be patted to about a 1/4- to 1/2-inch thickness, into strips about 1 inch wide and 8 inches long. Fold in half in the middle and twist the ends together to make a spiral.

Olliebollen, Olykoek (Dutch Fruit-Filled Doughnuts)

1 cup milk, scalded	3½ cups sifted flour
1 teaspoon salt	brandied raisins (see following
¼ cup sugar	recipe)
3 tablespoons butter	oil for deep frying
1 package dry yeast	confectioners' sugar
1 egg, well beaten	

Place the milk, salt, sugar, and 1 tablespoon of butter in a mixing bowl. Sprinkle on the yeast and proof for 10 minutes. Stir in the egg, remaining butter, and 1½ cups flour to make a stiff batter. Beat well. Gradually stir in remaining flour.

Turn onto a floured board and knead until smooth and elastic, adding more flour if required. Place the dough in a buttered bowl and cover with a sheet of plastic wrap and a towel. Set in a warm place and let rise until doubled in bulk, 2 to 3 hours. Punch down and knead again.

Cut off small pieces of dough about 2 tablespoons in size. Shape into balls and poke a dent in the center of each one. Put ¼ to ½ teaspoon of brandied raisins in each hole and pinch edges together to enclose the raisins in the balls. (Or, instead of putting fruit in the center, you can mix it into the dough.) Let rise on a lightly floured tray until doubled in bulk, about 20 minutes.

Heat oil to 375° F.

Fry balls until golden, about 3 minutes. Roll in confectioners' sugar while still warm. Can be frozen.

Yields about 36 doughnuts.

Note: You can also fill the doughnuts with a mixture of ½ cup dried currants, ¼ cup seedless raisins, ¼ cup chopped candied orange peel, and 2 tablespoons grated lemon peel.

BRANDIED RAISINS   Soak 1 cup of raisins in just enough brandy to cover for 24 hours to 4 months. Can be used as a dessert topping or in cakes as well.

Jelly Doughnuts

2 packages dry yeast	1 teaspoon grated lemon rind
2 tablespoons sugar	3 to 4 cups flour
1 teaspoon salt	1/4 cup soft butter
1 cup warm milk	fat for deep frying
1 egg	1 1/2 cups jam
2 egg yolks	sugar

Soften the yeast in 1/4 cup warm water. Add the sugar and salt. Cover and proof for 10 minutes. Stir in the milk, egg, egg yolks, and lemon rind and mix well. Add enough flour to make a medium firm dough. Work in the soft butter. Knead the dough until smooth and elastic. This can be done in a large processor, if desired. Place the kneaded dough into a bowl and dust lightly with flour. Cover the bowl with plastic wrap and a dish towel. Set in a warm place to double in bulk.

Punch the dough down, cover, and let rise a second time. Punch down and divide the dough into 36 pieces. Shape into smooth, slightly flattened balls and place on a floured towel. Let rise until doubled in bulk.

Heat the oil to 375° F.

Fry a few pieces of dough at a time until golden brown on the bottom. Turn and fry the second side until browned. Remove from the fat and drain on paper toweling. When completely cooled, fill the doughnuts with jam by forcing it through a long-nosed pastry tube (often sold as a Bismarck tube). Roll in sugar and serve.

These can be frozen before filling and coating with sugar.

Yields about 36.

OTHER SHAPES   You can shape this dough into small balls and deep fry as nuggets. Roll in sugar before serving. You can also roll the dough on a lightly floured board and cut out like standard doughnuts. Let rise until doubled in bulk and fry until golden on both sides. These can be glazed with an icing made of water and confectioners' sugar. (See page 166.) This glaze should be very thin. Let doughnuts drain on a cake rack for an hour or two to dry the coating.

Popovers

2 eggs
1 cup of milk
1 cup flour

¼ teaspoon salt
1 tablespoon melted butter

Preheat oven to 450° F.

Generously butter 6 custard cups or a popover pan. Put into preheated oven while preparing the batter.

In a processor, combine the eggs, milk, flour, salt, and butter. Process for 30 to 40 seconds. Fill custard cups no more than ⅔ full. Bake in the center of the oven for 20 minutes. Lower heat to 350° F. and bake 10 to 15 minutes longer, or until puffed and cooked.

Can be frozen after baking.

Yields 6.

Berry Muffins

2 cups sifted flour
1 tablespoon baking powder
3 tablespoons sugar
½ teaspoon salt
1 egg, beaten

1 cup milk
3 tablespoons melted butter
1 cup blueberries, pitted cherries, or other fruit tossed in ½ cup flour

Preheat the oven to 400° F.

Butter 12 2½-inch muffin tins.

In a medium bowl, mix together the flour, baking powder, sugar, and salt. Beat in the egg, milk, and butter until well blended. Do not overbeat. Toss the fruit with the flour and stir into the batter. Fill muffin tins ⅔ full. Bake for 20 to 30 minutes, or until golden and they test clean. Remove from the oven and unmold onto a cake rack. Serve warm.

Can be frozen after baking.

Yields 12.

Bran Muffins

2 tablespoons butter
¼ cup sugar
1 egg, well beaten
1 cup bran

¾ cup milk
1 cup flour
2½ teaspoons baking powder
pinch of salt

Preheat the oven to 400° F.

Butter 12 2½-inch muffin cups.

Cream the butter and sugar in a medium bowl until light and fluffy. Beat in the egg until well mixed. Mixture should look curdled. Combine the bran and the milk and stir into the egg mixture. Mix the flour, baking powder, and salt together well and stir into the bran mixture until all the ingredients are just moistened. Do not overmix.

Turn into muffin pan. Bake for 25 to 30 minutes, or until the muffins are brown and pull away from the sides of the pan. Serve warm.

Can be frozen and reheated.

Yields 12.

Muffin Variations

BANANA BRAN MUFFINS   Fold 3 bananas, finely diced, into the mixture along with the dry ingredients.

BLUEBERRY BRAN MUFFINS   Fold ½ cup washed blueberries into the mixture with the dry ingredients.

RAISIN BRAN MUFFINS   Substitute dark brown sugar for the white sugar and stir in ¾ cup seedless raisins with the dry ingredients.

Gingerbread Muffins

1 cup butter	1½ teaspoons baking soda
¼ cup brown sugar	1 teaspoon cinnamon
¼ cup sugar	1 teaspoon ground ginger
1 egg	¾ teaspoon salt
1 cup molasses	½ teaspoon ground cloves
3 cups flour, sifted	1 cup hot water

Preheat oven to 350° F.

Butter 12 muffin cups.

In medium bowl, cream butter and sugars until light. Beat in the egg and molasses. In a bowl, combine the flour, baking soda, cinnamon, ginger, salt, and cloves. Mix well and stir into the creamed butter alternately with the hot water, until the mixture is blended.

Spoon into muffin cups and bake until browned and the muffins start to pull away from the sides of the pan, about 25 minutes. Serve with butter.

Can be frozen.

Yields 12.

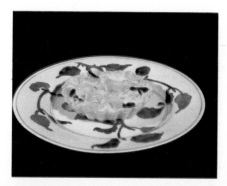

Asparagus Pie
(See page 141.)

Espadon en Brochettes
Swordfish on Skewers
(See page 129.)

Carrot Tart
(See page 142.)

Broiled Marinated Scallops
(See page 122.)

Seafood Crepes, Brandy's
(See page 110.)

Beef and Sausage with
Curried Noodles
(See page 92.)

Curried Shrimp
(See page 129.)

Oeufs Farcis a la Hollandaise
Stuffed Eggs with Hollandaise
(See page 47.)

Above
Shirred Eggs Borrachos
(See page 60.)

Princess Omelet
(See page 77.)

Above
Souffle au Fromage
et Jambon
*Souffle with Ham and
Cheese*
(See page 93.)

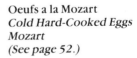

Oeufs a la Mozart
*Cold Hard-Cooked Eggs
Mozart*
(See page 52.)

Mushroom, Onion, and
Sausage Quiche
(See page 102.)

Coquilles St. Jacques au
Gratin
*Scallops with Mushroom
Duxelles*
(See page 122.)

Scrambled Eggs with Snail Toasts
(See page 71.)

Above
La Piperade du Pays Basque
Basque Pepper Omelet
(See page 85.)

Artichoke and Sausage
Deep Custard Pie
(See page 102.)

Oeufs Poches Aurore
Poached Eggs Aurora
(See page 39.)

BISCUITS

Baking powder biscuits, like doughnuts, are one of the trickier pastries to make. Although the ingredients are simple and easy to prepare, you must use a light hand or you will have heavy, hard biscuits. Careful, light handling will reward you with a truly delicious quick bread.

Baking Powder Biscuits

2 cups flour, sifted
2 teaspoons baking powder
1/2 teaspoon salt

1/4 cup butter, cut into pieces
3/4 cup milk

Preheat the oven to 450° F.

In a medium bowl, combine the flour, baking powder, and salt. Mix well. With your fingers or a pastry blender, cut in the butter as if making pie pastry. This can be done in a processor. The mixture will look like coarse meal. With a fork, quickly and lightly blend in the milk to make soft, slightly damp dough. Do not try to make the dough smooth.

Turn the dough onto a lightly floured board. With lightly floured hands, gently push it onto itself about four or five times. Pat out to a 1/2 inch thickness. Your hands will do just as well as a rolling pin. Cut into 2-inch squares or rounds and place on a lightly buttered baking sheet. Bake for 15 minutes, until puffed and golden brown on the top. Serve immediately or freeze as soon as they reach room temperature.

Yields about 24.

Note: Biscuits can be flavored with other ingredients and can also be shaped differently.

CHEESE BISCUITS   Add 1 cup grated Parmesan to the dry ingredients. You can use cheddar, if desired.

MUSTARD CHEESE BISCUITS   Add 1 tablespoon dry mustard and 1 cup grated cheddar to the dry ingredients. Shape and sprinkle cheese on top. This dough can also be baked in a 9 by 5 by 3 buttered loaf pan at 375° F. for 45 to 50 minutes. Cool in the pan for 10 minutes.

CINNAMON ROLLS   Add 1 tablespoon sugar, 1 teaspoon cinnamon, 1/4 teaspoon nutmeg, and a pinch of ground cloves to the dry ingredients. Make the dough and turn onto a lightly floured board. Roll into a rectangle 1/4 inch thick. Dot the surface with 8 tablespoons softened butter. In a bowl, combine 4 tablespoons sugar, 1 teaspoon cinnamon, and 1/4 teaspoon nutmeg. Mix well.

Sprinkle over the buttered pastry and roll into a jelly roll. Cut into 1 inch slices and place cut side down on a buttered baking sheet. Bake at 375° F. for 25 to 30 minutes, or until golden.

CINNAMON ROLL VARIATIONS   Add 1 cup chopped walnuts, pecans, or raisins to pastry before rolling. Or add both nuts and raisins to the pastry before rolling.

Buttermilk Chive Biscuits

3 cups sifted flour	2 tablespoons minced chives
2 tablespoons baking powder	1 cup butter
1 tablespoon sugar	¾ cup buttermilk
½ teaspoon baking soda	

Preheat oven to 400° F.

In a large bowl, combine the flour, baking powder, sugar, baking soda, and chives. Mix well. Cut in the butter until the mixture resembles coarse meal. Stir in the buttermilk and knead lightly on a floured board. Press on a buttered baking sheet into a 4 by 6 inch rectangle. Cut into squares but do not separate. Bake about 20 minutes, or until risen and golden.

Serve immediately, or freeze as soon as cool. As with any baking powder biscuit, you must handle the dough gently.

Yields about 24.

Corn Bread

1 cup yellow cornmeal	4 teaspoons baking powder
1 cup sifted flour	1 egg, lightly beaten
¼ cup sugar, optional	1 cup milk
½ teaspoon salt	¼ cup melted butter

Preheat oven to 375° F.

Butter an 8-inch square pan.

In a bowl, combine the cornmeal, flour, sugar, salt, and baking powder. Mix well. Mix in the egg, milk, and butter. Beat until well mixed, but do not overbeat. Pour into prepared pan and bake 30 minutes.

Serve immediately or freeze as soon as cool.

Yields 12 servings.

CORN MUFFINS Pour the mixture into 12 buttered muffin cups and bake for about 15 minutes.

CHEESE CORNBREAD Add 1½ cups grated cheddar to the dry ingredients.

HERBED CORNBREAD Add 1 teaspoon dried oregano and 1 teaspoon dried basil to the dry ingredients.

Anchovy Mozzarella Bread

2⅔ cups flour
 4 teaspoons baking powder
 ½ teaspoon salt
 4 ounces anchovies, diced

6 ounces grated mozzarella cheese
2 eggs
1 cup milk
2 tablespoons sugar

Preheat oven to 350° F.
Butter a 9 by 5 by 3 inch loaf pan.
In a bowl, combine the flour, baking powder, and salt. Mix well. Add the anchovies and mozzarella to the dry ingredients. Mix. Make a well in the dry ingredients and add the eggs, milk, and sugar. Mix the dough, breaking the egg yolks, until all ingredients are well moistened. Do not beat or overwork the dough. Pour into the prepared pan and bake for 1 hour. Cool to room temperature before serving.
Can be frozen.
Yields 1 loaf.

Salami Cheese Loaf

  3 cups flour
  2 tablespoons sugar
1½ tablespoons baking powder
1½ teaspoons salt
  1 teaspoon fennel seeds
  ¼ teaspoon baking soda
  3 tablespoons grated Parmesan
    cheese

11 ounces cream cheese, softened
 1 cup milk
 2 eggs, lightly beaten
 ¼ cup oil
 1 cup diced hard salami

Preheat oven to 375° F.

Butter a 9 by 5 by 3 inch loaf pan.

In a large bowl, mix the flour, sugar, baking powder, salt, fennel seeds, and baking soda together. Stir in the Parmesan.

With an electric mixer, cream the cheese until smooth and gradually beat in the milk to make a smooth mixture. Add eggs, oil, and salami. Mix well. Stir the cream cheese mixture into the dry ingredients until well moistened. Do not overbeat; the mixture should be lumpy.

Pour into the prepared pan and bake 1 hour, or until a cake tester inserted in the center comes out clean. Cool in the pan for 5 minutes. Serve warm.

Can be frozen after baking. Reheat before serving, if possible.

Yields 1 loaf.

Note: Can be used cold, thinly sliced, for sandwiches.

Oatmeal Raisin Bread

2 cups whole wheat flour	3 eggs, lightly beaten
2 cups rolled oats	2 tablespoons baking soda
2 cups buttermilk	2 tablespoons baking powder
1½ cups raisins	
1 cup firmly packed, light brown sugar	

Preheat oven to 350° F.

Generously butter a 9 by 5 by 3 inch loaf pan.

In a bowl, combine the flour, rolled oats, buttermilk, raisins, sugar, eggs, baking soda, and baking powder. Mix well until fully moistened, but do not overbeat. Fill loaf pan ¾ full and bake 1 hour, or until a toothpick inserted in the center comes out clean. Cool in pan for 5 minutes. Unmold and cool on wire rack.

Can be frozen.

Yields 1 loaf.

Apricot Nut Bread

½ cup dried apricots, diced
1 cup water
2 cups flour
½ cup sugar
2 tablespoons baking powder
1 teaspoon baking soda
1 teaspoon nutmeg

1 teaspoon cinnamon
½ teaspoon salt
¾ cup chopped walnuts
1 cup sour milk, or buttermilk
1 egg, lightly beaten
3 tablespoons melted butter

Preheat oven to 350° F.

Butter a 9 by 5 by 3 inch loaf pan.

In a small saucepan, simmer apricots in the water until the liquid is absorbed.

In a large bowl, mix together the flour, sugar, baking powder, baking soda, nutmeg, cinnamon, salt, and nuts. Beat in the milk, egg, and butter until blended completely. Pour into the prepared pan. Bake about 1 hour and 15 minutes, or until a toothpick inserted in the center comes out clean.

Can be frozen.

Yields 1 loaf.

APRICOT BRAN BREAD   Omit the nutmeg and cinnamon from the previous recipe and add 1 cup of bran to the dry ingredients.

Bourbon Pecan Bread

½ cup butter
½ cup dark brown sugar
2 large eggs
2½ teaspoons baking powder
2 cups flour

salt to taste
½ cup maple syrup
½ cup bourbon
1½ cups chopped pecans
confectioners' sugar

Preheat oven to 350° F.

Butter a 9½-inch tube pan.

Cream the butter in a medium bowl and beat in the sugar. Add the eggs, one at a time, beating well after each addition.

In a bowl, combine the baking powder, flour, and salt. Beat into the creamed butter alternating with the maple syrup and the bourbon. Stir in the pecans.

Pour into prepared pan. Bake 45 to 50 minutes, or until a toothpick inserted in the center comes out clean. Cool 10 minutes in the pan, remove from the pan, and cool. Serve sprinkled with confectioners' sugar, if desired.

Can be frozen.

Yields 1 cake.

Lemon Nut Bread

1½ cups flour	salt
1 teaspoon baking powder	½ cup chopped walnuts
2 eggs, lightly beaten	grated zest of 1 lemon
¼ pound butter, melted	juice of 1 large lemon
1 cup sugar	⅓ cup sugar

Preheat oven to 350° F.

Butter an 8½ by 4½ by 2½ inch loaf pan.

In a bowl, combine the flour and baking powder. Mix well. Add the eggs, butter, 1 cup sugar, salt, nuts, and lemon zest and beat together well. Pour into the pan and bake for 50 minutes or until a toothpick inserted in the center comes out clean.

For the glaze, mix the lemon juice and ⅓ cup sugar in a small bowl until the sugar is dissolved. Let the bread sit in the pan for 5 minutes, then pour the glaze over the top. Let stand in the pan another 10 minutes. Unmold.

Can be frozen.

Yields 1 loaf.

Orange Tea Bread

1 teaspoon butter	1 tablespoon baking powder
¾ cup sugar	1 cup milk
1 egg, lightly beaten	grated rind of 2 oranges
3 cups flour	

Preheat oven to 350° F.

Butter a 9 by 5 by 3 inch loaf pan.

In a bowl, cream the butter and sugar until light and fluffy. Beat in the egg.

In a bowl, mix the flour and baking powder together until well mixed. Add to the butter mixture along with the milk. Stir to combine ingredients.

Stir in the orange rind. Pour into prepared pan. Bake for about 50 minutes, or until a toothpick inserted in the center comes out clean.

Can be frozen.

Yields 1 loaf.

Swedish Coffee Cake

¼ cup butter	2 eggs, separated
1 cup sugar	½ cup milk
1½ cups flour	½ cup sugar
1 teaspoon salt	1 teaspoon cinnamon
2 teaspoons baking powder	¼ cup chopped pecans, or walnuts

Preheat oven to 350° F.

Butter a 9-inch layer cake pan.

In a mixer, cream the butter and 1 cup sugar until light and fluffy.

In a small bowl, mix together the flour, salt, and baking powder. Combine the egg yolks and milk. Add the flour and egg mixtures to the butter alternately, mixing completely.

Beat the egg whites until stiff but not dry and fold into the batter. Pour into the pan.

In a small bowl, combine the remaining sugar, cinnamon, and nuts. Sprinkle over the top of the cake. Bake for about 40 minutes, or until a toothpick inserted in the center comes out clean.

Can be frozen.

Yields 1 cake.

Budapest Coffee Cake

⅔ cup packed dark brown sugar	1½ teaspoons baking soda
1 tablespoon cinnamon	½ teaspoon salt
1 tablespoon unsweetened cocoa	¾ cup butter
2 to 3 tablespoons currants, chopped	2 teaspoons vanilla
½ cup chopped walnuts	1½ cups sugar
3 cups sifted flour	3 eggs
1½ tablespoons baking powder	2 cups sour cream
	vanilla icing (see following recipe)

Preheat oven to 375° F.

Butter a 10-inch turban mold or Bundt pan.

In a bowl, combine the brown sugar, cinnamon, cocoa, currants, and walnuts. Mix well and set aside.

In a medium bowl, combine the flour, baking powder, baking soda, and salt. Mix well.

Cream the butter, vanilla, and sugar until light and fluffy. Beat in the eggs, one at a time, beating well after each addition. Fold the dry ingredients into the creamed mixture alternately with the sour cream.

Spread a thin layer of the batter in the bottom of the pan and sprinkle generously with ⅓ of the nut filling. Continue to layer, finishing with the batter. If you have difficulty spreading the batter, drop it by small spoonfuls. Bake for 55 to 60 minutes, or until a toothpick inserted in the center comes out clean. Let cool in the pan for 5 minutes, then unmold. Serve plain or glaze with vanilla icing.

Can be frozen.

Yields 1 cake.

VANILLA ICING   Combine 2 cups confectioners' sugar, 1 teaspoon vanilla, and 2 to 3 tablespoons milk. Beat until smooth. If necessary, add more milk to make a glaze about the thickness of cream sauce. Drizzle over the cake while still warm, letting it run down the sides.

CHAPTER 11
Yeast Breads, Coffee Cakes, and Pastries

It is possible to have a brunch without breads, but not as satisfying. This is the time to indulge a love of coffee cakes, Danish pastries, brioche, and croissants. Although delicious pastries can sometimes be purchased, the one certain way to serve fine breads is to make them yourself. They are not difficult.

Yeast breads, which generally seem the most frightening to make, in fact are the easiest. Yeast breads can be made ahead and frozen with great success.

Although recipes for yeast breads seem to require a lot of time, it is time that does not involve the baker. Letting the dough rise somewhat longer or shorter than specified is not a serious problem. There are two things that can result in failure—if the yeast is killed during the initial stages, or if the kneading is not vigorous and long enough.

Yeast is a living organism and needs a warm, humid atmosphere in which to grow. If it is too hot, however, the yeast dies. Generally, it should be mixed with ingredients no hotter than 100° F. to 110° F. (comfortably warm to the touch). If it is too hot for you, it is too hot for the yeast. The bread rises, ideally, at 85° F. to 90° F. It will rise at lower temperatures, but it will take longer. This fact can be an asset, however, since the longer, slower rise helps flavor to develop. Some breads can be left to rise overnight in a refrigerator.

Kneading is a simple process and comforting to do. Once you have learned how, you develop a rhythm that makes kneading truly enjoyable. Underkneading can result in a heavy loaf, but it is virtually impossible to overknead. Some electric mixers are capable of kneading, and many breads can be kneaded in a food processor. Unless you are rushed, however, take the time to enjoy kneading by hand.

Brioche

4 packages dry yeast	4 cups flour, or more
¼ cup sugar	1 cup softened butter
2 teaspoons salt	2 egg yolks
¾ cup warm milk	2 teaspoons cream, or milk
6 egg yolks, or 3 whole eggs	

In a bowl, proof the yeast by dissolving it in ½ cup lukewarm water. Stir in the sugar and salt to make a syrup. Add the milk and the 6 egg yolks, or 3 eggs. Stir well. Beat in 3 cups of flour and the softened butter.

Knead this moist sticky dough thoroughly. If you have a heavy-duty mixer that kneads, this is the time to use it. If you are kneading by hand, leave the ingredients in the bowl and knead as follows. Pick up the dough and slap it down into the bowl. Keep stretching and slapping it between the bowl and your fingers. The dough is ready when it is firm and elastic, with bubbles on the surface, and it no longer sticks to your hands.

Add up to 2 more cups of flour, if required, to make a satiny smooth dough. Place the kneaded dough in a bowl, dust lightly with flour, and cover with plastic wrap and a towel. Let rise until doubled in bulk, about 1 hour. Punch down and let rise again. Chill the dough for at least two hours to make shaping easier.

Preheat oven to 400° F.

Butter 16 small brioche molds (about 3 inches across the top) or 1 large mold. Cut the dough into 2-ounce pieces and divide these into 1½-ounce and ½-ounce sections. Shape the larger piece into a compact ball in the palms of your hands and place in the mold. With your finger, poke a deep hole in the center. Shape the smaller piece into a tear drop and insert into the hole. Let rise until they come to the tops of the tins and are doubled in bulk.

In a small bowl, combine the egg yolks and cream. Brush the brioche with the mixture and bake for about 20 minutes, or until they are a deep, dark brown and start to pull from the sides of the molds. A large brioche bakes in about 60 minutes.

Can be frozen.

Yields about 16 small brioche, or 1 large brioche.

VARIATIONS   Brioche can be flavored with cinnamon or nutmeg; or beat in brandied raisins or other fruits mentioned in the recipe for Olliebollen in chapter 10.

SHAPES   Brioche, the classic French breakfast bread, is not difficult to make and it can be made in any shape. The traditional fluted mold is the size and shape most associated with brioche, but you can use custard cups, muffin tins, or any other small mold to shape individual brioche. One of the popular shapes seen in France is a tall round loaf, which you can duplicate by baking the loaf in a coffee tin. Prepare the tin with a collar like a souffle (see page 88), and fill the can ⅔ full. Brioche can be baked in a 9 by 5 inch bread pan, a round cake pan, or even a tube pan (plain or in the shape of a Turk's head mold). If well-chilled, the dough can also be braided and baked on a buttered baking sheet.

Honey Bran Bread

2 packages dry yeast
¼ cup warm water
1 cup milk, scalded
2 teaspoons butter, softened
1 teaspoon salt

½ cup honey
3 tablespoons sugar
1½ cups bran
3½ cups flour

Dissolve the yeast in the water. Combine the milk, butter, salt, honey, and sugar, and mix well. Stir in the yeast with the bran and 3 cups of flour. Mix well.

Turn onto a lightly floured board and knead the dough until it is relatively smooth and elastic. Place in a buttered bowl, turning to coat the surface. Cover with plastic wrap and a towel and let rise for about 2 hours, or until doubled in bulk.

Preheat oven to 350° F.

Butter a 9 by 5 by 3 inch loaf pan. Punch dough down, place in pan, and let rise until doubled in bulk. Bake for 50 to 60 minutes, or until it sounds hollow on the bottom when tapped. Cool at least 20 minutes before slicing.

Can be frozen.

Yields 1 loaf.

La Fouace aux Noix (Walnut Hearth Bread)

3½ to 4 cups unbleached flour
½ cup whole wheat flour
1 package dry yeast
1 tablespoon salt
1 cup warm milk

⅓ cup warm water
1 cup coarsely chopped walnuts
¾ cup minced onion
½ cup unsalted butter, softened
2 tablespoons cornmeal

In a medium bowl, combine 1¾ cups of unbleached flour, whole wheat flour, yeast, and salt. Mix well. Add the milk and water and beat for 3 minutes. Stir in the walnuts, onion, and butter and mix well. Blend and knead in the remaining flour to make a stiff dough. Place in a buttered bowl, turning to coat the surface. Cover with plastic wrap and a towel and let rise until doubled in bulk.

Sprinkle a baking sheet or pie plate with the cornmeal, just in the area the bread will cover. Punch down the dough and knead for 3 to 4 minutes. Shape into a ball and place on the cornmeal. Let rise uncovered.

Preheat oven to 425° F.

When the bread has risen for 30 minutes, use a razor blade to slash the top. Make a simple *x*, cut a square, or cut swirling lines that converge at one side of the loaf. Place a pan of hot water on the lowest rack of the oven. Place the bread on the middle rack and bake for 30 minutes. Remove the water, lower the heat to 300° F., and bake for 30 minutes longer. Cool on a rack.

Can be frozen.

Yields 1 loaf.

Garlic Potato Bread

1 large potato, boiled, cooled, and grated (about 1½ cups)
1 teaspoon salt
1 large clove garlic, crushed
1 cup warm water from cooking potato
1 package dry yeast
2 teaspoons sugar
2 cups flour
softened butter

In a bowl, combine the potato, salt, garlic, potato water, yeast, and sugar. Mix well. Stir in the flour and mix again. Turn the dough onto a board and knead until smooth. Place in a buttered bowl and turn to coat the surface. Cover with plastic wrap and a towel. Let rise until doubled in bulk, about 1 hour.

Punch the dough down and shape into a ball. Place on a baking sheet sprinkled with flour or cornmeal where the bread will sit. Or bake the bread in an 8- or 9-inch skillet with an ovenproof handle. Brush the bread with butter and let rise until doubled in bulk.

Preheat oven to 450° F.

Bake for 25 to 30 minutes, or until golden brown.

Can be frozen.

Yields 1 loaf.

Sausage Bread

1 pound sausage links
2 packages dry yeast
¼ cup warm water
1 tablespoon sugar
1 cup warm milk
¼ cup butter, softened
1 teaspoon salt
3 eggs, lightly beaten
5 cups flour

Cut the sausages into 1-inch lengths and place in a 1-quart saucepan with water to cover. Simmer 10 minutes. Drain and saute in a 9-inch skillet until cooked.

In a large bowl, sprinkle the yeast over the water and stir well. Let proof until foamy. Stir in the sugar, milk, butter, salt, and eggs. Stir in 2 cups of flour and beat well. Stir in the remaining flour. The dough will look very rough. Turn the dough onto a lightly floured board and knead until smooth. Place the dough in a buttered bowl, turning to coat the surface. Cover with plastic wrap and a towel and let rise until double in bulk.

Punch the dough down and knead gently. Sprinkle half of the sausage onto the dough and knead it in until uniform. Divide the dough into two pieces and shape into flat, round loaves. Place on buttered pie plates, or on a buttered baking sheet. Let rise until doubled in bulk.

Preheat oven to 375° F.

Place the remaining sausage on the loaves. Bake for 40 minutes.

Can be frozen.

Yields 2 loaves.

Orange Raisin Bread

1½ cups warm water	4½ cups sifted flour
2 packages dry yeast	½ cup seedless raisins
½ cup sugar	1 egg yolk
1 teaspoon salt	½ cup light brown sugar, packed
¼ cup butter, softened	2 tablespoons grated orange rind
1 egg plus 1 egg white	3 tablespoons chopped pecans
2 tablespoons grated orange rind	

In a medium bowl, sprinkle the yeast over the water and let proof. Stir to dissolve. Add the sugar, salt, butter, egg, egg white, 2 tablespoons orange rind, and 3 cups of flour. Beat until smooth. Stir in the raisins and the rest of the flour. Place in a buttered bowl, turning to coat the surface. Cover the bowl and let rise in a warm place for about 1 hour, or until light and bubbly and more than double in bulk.

Lightly butter a 2-quart souffle dish. Stir down the dough and beat vigorously for 1 minute. Turn into the prepared dish. Brush the top of the loaf with the egg yolk.

In a bowl, combine the brown sugar, remaining orange rind, and pecans. Sprinkle over the loaf. Let rise for 30 minutes, or until almost doubled in bulk.

Preheat oven to 375° F.

Bake for 55 minutes. Remove from the casserole and cool on a rack. Can be frozen.

Yields 1 loaf.

Eastern European Nut Roll

3 packages dry yeast	2 egg yolks
½ cup lukewarm water	5 cups flour
½ cup sugar	3 eggs
¾ cup milk, warmed	½ cup sugar
½ cup butter, softened	2 cups grated walnuts
1 teaspoon salt	½ cup melted butter
grated rind of 1 lemon	grated rind of 2 oranges
1 teaspoon vanilla	½ teaspoon cinnamon
2 eggs	icing (see following recipe)

In a large bowl, sprinkle the yeast on the water and let proof. Add ½ cup sugar, milk, soft butter, salt, lemon rind, and vanilla to the yeast. Mix well. Beat in the 2 eggs and egg yolks. Stir in 2 cups of flour and beat well. Gradually add enough remaining flour to make a smooth, pliable dough. Turn out onto a board and knead for 10 minutes, adding flour if needed, until the dough is smooth and elastic. Gather into a ball and place in a floured bowl. Dust the top with flour and cover with a towel. Let rise until doubled in bulk, about 1 to 1½ hours.

Butter 2 9-inch loaf pans. Punch the dough down and knead for 3 minutes. In a medium bowl, beat the 3 eggs with ½ cup sugar until thick and pale. Stir in the nuts, melted butter, orange rind, and cinnamon. Roll the dough into a large rectangle ⅓ inch thick. Spread the filling over the surface and roll up. Cut the roll in half and place in loaf pans. Let rise until doubled in bulk.

Preheat oven to 350° F.

Brush loaves with lukewarm water. Bake for about 45 minutes, or until golden. Cool before icing.

Can be frozen.

Yields 1 loaf.

Note: If the nut rolls are to be frozen, frost after thawing.

ICING

1 cup confectioners' sugar	orange juice

In a bowl, combine the sugar with enough orange juice to make a runny icing. Drizzle over the nut rolls.

Kugelhopf (Almond Raisin Coffee Cake)

1 package dry yeast	1 cup warm milk
1/4 cup warm water	2 cups flour
1/2 teaspoon salt	1/4 pound seedless raisins
1 tablespoon sugar	1/2 cup ground almonds
1/3 cup butter, softened	almond halves for decoration
2 eggs, lightly beaten	

In a large bowl, dissolve the yeast in the water with the salt and sugar. Let proof. Beat in the butter, eggs, milk, and flour to make a dough. Knead the dough in the bowl until satiny smooth and bubbles appear on the surface (about 10 minutes of vigorous kneading). Knead in the raisins.

Butter a 9-inch turban mold and dust with ground almonds. Place almond halves on the bottom of the mold in a decorative pattern. Add the dough and let rise until it reaches the top of the mold.

Preheat oven to 400° F.

Bake for 40 to 45 minutes, or until nicely browned. A toothpick inserted in the center should come out clean. Unmold and cool on a rack.

Can be frozen.

Yields 1 cake.

Note: Kugelhopfs are often served dusted with confectioners' sugar, but they can also be glazed with rum or chocolate frosting.

PROCESSOR METHOD Add all ingredients, except raisins and almonds, to the processor bowl. Process to a smooth, satiny dough. Turn onto a lightly floured surface and knead in the raisins.

RUM FROSTING

1 cup confectioners' sugar	1 tablespoon dark rum

In a bowl, combine the sugar and rum, adding more rum if needed to make a thin frosting. Drizzle over the cooled cake and let it run down the sides.

CHOCOLATE ICING

7 ounces semisweet chocolate	1 cup confectioners' sugar
5 tablespoons butter	4 tablespoons cold water

In the top of a double boiler, over hot but not boiling water, melt the chocolate and stir in the butter. Remove from the heat and let cool to lukewarm. Sift the sugar and stir into the chocolate with the water. If the icing is too hot, it will roll off the cake; if it is not hot enough, it will not spread evenly.

Rich Sour Cream Dough

This dough can be shaped and filled in several ways (see the following recipes).

4 packages dry yeast
½ cup sugar
1 teaspoon salt
½ cup cold milk
1 cup sour cream

2 teaspoons lemon juice
1 teaspoon vanilla
3 egg yolks
5 to 6 cups flour
1½ cups butter, softened

In a large bowl, dissolve the yeast in ½ cup warm water. Stir in the sugar and salt and let proof. Stir in the milk, sour cream, lemon juice, vanilla, and egg yolks. Add enough flour to make a medium firm dough. Beat in the butter. Turn onto a lightly floured board and knead, adding more flour as required to make a smooth, elastic dough.

Let rise in the refrigerator for at least 4 hours. The dough can remain in the refrigerator at this stage for up to 3 days. Punch it down whenever it comes close to doubling in bulk.

Butter Twists

1 recipe rich sour cream dough
  made with only 1 tablespoon
  sugar

2 to 3 cups granulated sugar

On a lightly floured board, roll the chilled dough into a rectangle about ⅓ inch thick. Sprinkle generously with sugar. Fold the dough in thirds, like a business letter. Wrap in floured foil or parchment paper and refrigerate for 20 minutes.

Place the pastry with one of the open ends facing you and roll again to a ⅓ inch thickness. Sprinkle with sugar and fold again. Chill. Repeat the procedure one more time.

Divide the dough in half and roll into 8 by 16 inch rectangles. Sprinkle with sugar and fold in half to make 4 by 16 inch rectangles. Cut into strips

1 inch wide and 4 inches long. Dip the strips in sugar, twist the ends, and chill for 30 minutes.

Preheat oven to 375° F.

Place the strips on ungreased baking sheets and press the ends down. Bake for 20 minutes, or until golden.

Can be frozen.

Yields 6 dozen.

CINNAMON TWISTS   Add 2 to 3 tablespoons of cinnamon, or to taste, to the sugar before rolling into the pastry.

NUT AND FRUIT TWISTS   Sprinkle the pastry with raisins and nuts, or candied fruits, to your taste before folding in half and cutting into strips.

Orange Honey Twists

1 recipe rich sour cream dough	⅔ cup chopped walnuts, or pecans
¼ cup melted butter	1 cup raisins
½ cup butter, softened	1 egg yolk
grated rind of 1 large orange	1 teaspoon heavy cream
⅔ cup honey	½ cup blanched sliced almonds

Preheat oven to 350° F.

Butter two 9 by 5 by 3 inch loaf pans, a single large baking sheet, or two 9-inch layer cake pans.

Roll the pastry into a large square ¼ inch thick. Brush with melted butter.

In a bowl, cream the soft butter, orange rind, honey, and walnuts. Spread over the dough and sprinkle with the raisins. Roll up jelly roll fashion. With a rolling pin, roll it to a 1 inch thickness. Cut into 3 strips lengthwise. Cut the strips in half horizontally and braid each 3 strips into a loaf. Place the loaves in the loaf pans, free form them on a baking sheet, or form rings in the layer pans.

In a small bowl, combine the egg yolk and cream and brush over the loaves. Sprinkle with the almonds. Bake about 45 minutes, or until golden. Remove from the pans and cool on a rack.

Can be frozen.

Yields 2 cakes.

VARIATIONS   This coffee cake can be filled like the Budapest coffee cake (page 165) or some of the Danish pastries (pages 177–180).

POPPY SEED FILLING

½ pound poppy seeds
½ cup butter
½ cup honey
1 teaspoon grated orange peel

2 tablespoons heavy cream
1 cup chopped walnuts
½ cup raisins

Put poppy seeds in a small bowl. Pour in enough boiling water to cover and let stand overnight. Drain well. Grind the poppy seeds 3 times with the finest blade of a meat grinder.

Cream the butter and honey. Add the poppy seeds, orange peel, cream, walnuts, and raisins. Use to fill coffee cakes.

CHEESE FILLING

¼ cup raisins
2 tablespoons cognac
1 cup cream cheese
¼ cup sugar
1 tablespoon flour

1 egg yolk
1 teaspoon melted butter
1 tablespoon sour cream
½ teaspoon grated lemon rind
½ teaspoon vanilla

Soak the raisins in the cognac for 20 minutes. Cream the cheese, sugar, and flour together. Stir in the egg yolk, butter, sour cream, lemon rind, and vanilla. Beat in the raisins and juices.

Croissants

1 package dry yeast
1 tablespoon sugar
½ cup warm water
4 cups flour

1 tablespoon salt
2 tablespoons sugar
1 cup cold milk, approximate
½ pound butter

In a small bowl, combine the yeast, 1 tablespoon sugar, and water. Mix and let proof.

In a large bowl, combine the flour, salt, and remaining sugar. Mix well. Make a well in the center and stir in the yeast mixture and milk. Working quickly and lightly, stir the ingredients together to make a rough, crumbly mass. Turn out onto the work counter. Let rest 5 minutes. Wash and dry the bowl.

With a pastry scraper or pancake turner, lift the dough up onto itself and press together gently 8 to 10 times. THIS IS ALL THE KNEADING YOU DO. Place in the bowl and let rise for 2 hours, or until doubled in bulk. Punch down.

Wrap the pastry in a plastic bag and shape into a flat, square brick about 1½ inches thick. Refrigerate for at least 20 minutes while you shape the butter.

Knead the butter to make it smooth, pliable, and waxy. One of the easiest ways to do this is to put it in a plastic bag and work it until the butter is the same consistency as the dough. If the butter gets too soft and is greasy, put it in the refrigerator to firm it. When it is kneaded sufficiently, roll the butter, while still in the bag, to about ¼ inch thick. The bag will help to shape it into an even rectangle. Refrigerate until firm, but not hard.

When chilled, cut the rectangle of butter in half. Roll the pastry on a lightly floured board into a long rectangle as wide as the butter and three times as long as one of the halves. Unwrap a half of butter and put it in the center of the dough. Pick up one end of pastry and place it over the butter. Place the second half of butter on the dough and cover with remaining end of the pastry. Try to keep all edges as square as possible.

Turn the pastry so that an open end faces you. Roll it into a long rectangle. Fold each end to the center. Fold in half again so that the dough resembles a book. Wrap in floured foil, or put in a plastic bag, and chill for at least 20 minutes. Roll and fold again. Let rest in the refrigerator for 3 hours.

Divide the pastry in half and roll each half into a large rectangle, about ¼ inch thick. Cut into triangles, about five inches on all sides. Roll up each triangle toward an opposite point, stretching the point slightly. Place on an unbuttered baking sheet, twisting in the ends to make a crescent. The center point should not rest under the croissant but should point down toward the pan. Let rise for 30 minutes.

Preheat oven to 400° F.

Brush the croissants with a *dorure* (see Glossary), or 1 egg yolk mixed with 1 tablespoon heavy cream. Bake croissants for 20 to 25 minutes, or until golden.

Can be frozen.

Yields about 36 croissants.

Copenhagen Yeast Dough

This makes a particularly light and flaky Danish pastry.

3½ cups flour	2 egg yolks
3 packages dry yeast	¼ cup sugar
1 cup milk	3 tablespoons butter
pinch of salt	⅛ teaspoon ground cardamom
1 egg	1½ cups butter

In a bowl, combine the flour, yeast, milk, salt, egg, egg yolks, sugar, 3 tablespoons butter, and a generous pinch of cardamom. Mix well until the mixture just holds together. Turn onto a board and knead 8 times, with a pastry scraper or pancake turner, by lifting and pressing the dough onto itself. Wrap in lightly floured foil or in a plastic bag. Shape into a cake about 5 inches square and 1 inch thick. Refrigerate for 20 minutes.

Work the remaining butter in a bowl of ice water, or in a plastic bag, until malleable, but not oily. Shape into a block, about ¾ inch thick.

Roll the pastry into a 12-inch square. Place the block of butter on it diagonally and bring the corners of the dough over the butter to meet in the center. Press edges together. Roll the pastry on a lightly floured board until it is three times longer than wide. Fold in thirds. Let rest 20 minutes. Roll and fold again, and let rest 1 hour. It is now ready to shape into pastries. Once the pastries are shaped, let them rise for 20 minutes.

Preheat oven to 400° F.

Bake until golden brown.

Can be frozen.

Yields 24 to 36 pastries.

Shapes and Flavors

For convenience, the author has combined a specific filling with a particular shape of pastry. In fact, these shapes and flavors can be interchanged at will.

Twists

2 cups almonds, toasted and ground	3 tablespoons milk
6 tablespoons sugar	pinch of cinnamon
½ cup fresh bread crumbs	½ teaspoon vanilla

In a bowl, combine the almonds, sugar, bread crumbs, milk, cinnamon, and vanilla. Mix well. If needed, add more milk to make the filling creamy.

Roll half of the pastry ¼ inch thick and spread filling thinly over one half of the dough. Fold in half to cover the filling and cut into ½-inch wide strips. Holding each strip by the ends, twist in opposite directions to form a spiral. Place on a buttered baking sheet. Use remaining pastry to make another shape or repeat.

Note: Can be glazed with rum frosting (see Kugelhopf recipe).

Pretzels

1 egg yolk
1 tablespoon cream

1 cup sliced or chopped almonds
vanilla icing (see recipe p. 166)

Roll half of the pastry ¼ inch thick. Cut into ½-inch wide strips and shape into pretzels. Brush with the egg wash (egg mixed with the cream) and dust with almonds. Let rise for at least 20 minutes, or until puffy looking. Bake until golden. Coat with vanilla icing.

Twin Rolls

1 cup shredded, toasted hazelnuts
1 cup cinnamon sugar

vanilla icing (see recipe p. 166)
egg wash (dorure, p. 208)

Roll half of the pastry ⅛ inch thick. Sprinkle with hazelnuts and cinnamon sugar. Roll like a jelly roll. Cut into 1-inch thick sections, cutting each section almost through to the bottom. Place on a buttered baking sheet and spread to show double roll. Brush with an egg wash (see Pretzels) and bake. Coat with vanilla icing.

Raspberry Stars

10 ounces raspberry jam

egg wash (dorure, p. 208)

Roll ¼ of pastry into a 12-inch wide strip, ⅛ inch thick. Spread with raspberry jam and roll like a jelly roll. Cut into ¾-inch thick sections and place, cut side down, on a buttered baking sheet. With scissors make six cuts in each piece, running from the outer edge to the center. Brush with an egg wash and bake.

Butterflies

10 ounces apricot jam
2 tablespoons grated lemon rind

lemon juice to taste
egg wash (dorure, p. 208)

Roll half of the pastry ¼ inch thick. Spread with apricot jam and sprinkle with lemon rind and lemon juice. Roll into a log. Cut into sections 1 inch thick. Holding the sections upright, use a thin piece of wood to press down the center top of each piece and spread it open to form a butterfly. Set on buttered baking sheets and brush with an egg wash.

Fans

---

filling for Orange Honey Twists
   (see page 175)
vanilla icing (see page 166)

egg wash (dorure, p. 208)

Roll the pastry 1 inch thick and 9 inches wide. Spread with orange honey filling. Fold in thirds so that the pastry is 3 inches wide. Cut crosswise into 2-inch wide sections. Make 3 small cuts on the long sides of each piece but not through the middle—like fringing both ends. Place on a baking sheet, twisting the pastry and spreading the sections. Brush with egg wash and bake. Coat with vanilla icing.

CHAPTER 12
Fruits

Dessert is not part of breakfast and is not necessarily part of brunch. But for those people who want something sweet, fruit can provide the solution. Of course, fruit also can be served as a first course. Years ago, the New England breakfast often included hot apple or blueberry pie. Today, hosts or hostesses may offer individual fruit tarts, or a simple and delicious fruit preparation that is quick to prepare. For example, a melon half or a bowl of berries, accompanied perhaps with cream and sugar, is often sufficient. However, there are also wonderful fruit compotes and macedoines, as well as other appropriate fruit preparations.

Many of these recipes can be prepared ahead, but fresh fruits, served simply, often must be eaten within a short time after preparation. Strawberries, once hulled, start to look less inviting within a few hours and should be served soon after preparing. The same warning applies to many fruits. Consider whether the fruit will turn brown quickly, like newly cut peaches, or look tired, like melons, if prepared several hours ahead.

When added to fruits, sugar syrup can draw out the juices and "cook" it in a certain way. Therefore, depending on whether you want fresh, vibrantly crisp fruit or syrup-coddled fruit, let the fruit macerate for a few minutes up to 24 hours before serving.

Fruit recipes are quite flexible. Macedoines and compotes list the fruits to be used, but you can make substitutions according to what is available. Recipes that use apples can use pears; berries can be interchanged. Use your imagination.

Macerated Fruits

⅔ cup dry vermouth, or orange juice	1 large pineapple, cut into chunks
5 tablespoons sugar	4 navel oranges, peeled and sectioned
½ teaspoon cinnamon	2 pears, diced

In a bowl, combine the vermouth, sugar, and cinnamon and let stand for one hour, stirring occasionally. Strain the liquid, discarding any undissolved sugar.

Prepare the fruits and place in a bowl. Pour the liquid over the fruits and macerate for at least 1 hour before serving.

Can be made the night before.

Serves 6.

Fruits Rafraichis au Kirsch (Fresh Fruits with Kirsch)

½ cup sugar
 1 cup water
 2 teaspoons lemon juice
pinch of salt
 2 apricots, peeled and quartered
½ cup fresh pineapple chunks

½ cup pitted cherries
½ cup strawberries, hulled
 2 nectarines, peeled and quartered
 2 to 3 tablespoons kirsch, Cointreau,
   or framboise

In a small saucepan, combine the sugar, water, lemon juice, and salt. Bring to a boil and simmer 5 minutes. Cool.

Place the prepared fruits in a bowl and pour the syrup on just before serving. Sprinkle with liqueur.

The fruits can be prepared the night before. Refrigerate in a bowl securely covered with plastic wrap.

Serves 6.

Macedoine de Fruits (Fresh Fruit Cup)

 1 small pineapple
½ pound fresh peaches
 1 pint strawberries
sugar, if needed

 1 teaspoon minced fresh ginger
 1 teaspoon minced lemon rind
¼ cup port

Peel and dice the fruits. Cut strawberries in half if large. Add sugar to the fruits if they need it. Stir in ginger, lemon rind, and port. Let macerate for at least 1 hour.

Can be made the night before.

Serves 6.

Macedoine de Fruits Rafraichis (Mixture of Fresh Fruits)

 3 oranges
 2 lemons
 2 limes
 5 cups sugar
3½ cups water
 1 teaspoon cream of tartar
 2 grapefruit
 1 small melon

 2 ripe pears
½ pound plums
 2 bananas
¼ pound cherries, pitted
 3 ripe peaches
¼ pound grapes
juice of 1 lemon
kirsch or Cointreau to taste

With a sharp knife or zester, remove just the colored portion of the rind of the oranges, lemons, and limes. Cut into fine julienne.

In a 2-quart saucepan, combine the sugar, water, and cream of tartar over low heat until the sugar has dissolved. Add the julienned rinds and simmer until the rinds are translucent, about 1 hour. Cool the rinds in the syrup. Store in a screw-top jar in a cupboard, not in the refrigerator. The syrup will keep for several months.

Peel and section the oranges and grapefruit. Cut the melon into cubes or balls. Peel the pears and slice. Cut plums into sections, discarding the pit. Peel the bananas, cut into thick slices, and toss in the lemon juice to prevent darkening. Peel and slice the peaches and toss in lemon juice to prevent darkening. Seed the grapes if necessary. (You may choose to peel the grapes.)

Layer the fruit in a serving bowl. Sprinkle with the liqueur but be judicious. Use just enough liqueur to enhance the flavors of the fruit, not overpower them. Cover with plastic wrap and chill overnight until serving time. Just before serving, spoon on a tablespoon or so of the rind and some of the syrup. Pass additional syrup on the side, if desired.

The syrup can be prepared months ahead. Prepare the fruits the night before. Do not add syrup until just before serving or juices will become watery.

Serves 6 to 8.

Note: A zester is a special utensil with 5 tiny round holes used to make julienned citrus peel. It is available in gourmet shops.

Compote of Fruits

2 cups sugar	½ cup dried peaches
5 cups water	½ cup dried pears
½ cup dried apricots	1 teaspoon vanilla
½ cup pitted prunes	½ cup slivered almonds, toasted
½ cup dried figs	

In a 3-quart saucepan, combine the sugar and water. Bring to a boil and simmer 5 minutes. Add the apricots, prunes, figs, peaches, and pears. Simmer until tender, about 20 minutes. Stir in the vanilla and the almonds. Serve warm, with heavy cream, or cold.

Serves 6 to 8.

Note: Use any variety of dried fruits you wish in this compote. You also can add a thinly sliced lemon to the fruits during poaching.

Gateau Campagnard (French Baked Apple Dessert)

1½ pounds apples, peeled and cored
¾ cup confectioners' sugar
¼ teaspoon nutmeg

2 cups flour
½ pound butter, softened
½ cup heavy cream, or more

Preheat oven to 400° F.

Cut the apples into ¼-inch thick slices. Butter a 9 by 13 inch baking dish and put the apples in the bottom. Sprinkle with the sugar and the nutmeg. Bake for 15 minutes.

In a medium bowl, mix the flour, butter, and enough cream to make a very soft dough. Pour the dough over the apples and bake for 45 minutes. Serve hot, warm, or cool.

Can be reheated.

Serves 6.

Apricots Fines Bouches (Apricots with Kirsch Sauce)

1 large can apricots
2 egg yolks
2 tablespoons kirsch

1 tablespoon sugar
6 tablespoons butter, softened
½ cup sliced almonds, toasted

Drain the apricots very well and arrange on a serving platter. Refrigerate.

In a 1-quart saucepan, combine the egg yolks, kirsch, and sugar. Set over medium heat and whisk until slightly thickened. Whisk in the butter, 1 tablespoon at a time, until the mixture is thick and creamy. Be careful not to overheat or the sauce will curdle. Pour the sauce over the apricots and sprinkle with almonds. Serve at room temperature.

Can be prepared the night before.

Serves 6.

Bananes Maltaise (Bananas with Orange)

6 bananas
2 tablespoons butter
6 tablespoons sugar

1 or 2 oranges
2 to 4 tablespoons Grand Marnier

Peel the bananas and cut in half lengthwise. In a 10-inch skillet, melt the butter and saute the bananas for 2 minutes on each side. Sprinkle with sugar and cook over high heat to caramelize the sugar lightly. Grate orange peel over the bananas. Squeeze the juice of the orange on top of the bananas and simmer until the juice is reduced to a syrup. Swirl in the Grand Marnier and ignite. Serve immediately.

Can be prepared to the point of adding the Grand Marnier, allowed to cool, and reheated.

Serves 6.

Bananes Caribe (Bananas and Oranges with Rum)

8 bananas
3 oranges, thinly sliced
½ cup brown sugar

½ cup butter
½ cup rum

Preheat oven to 300° F.

Peel and halve the bananas lengthwise. Arrange in a buttered baking dish in one layer. Cover the bananas with the orange slices and sprinkle on the brown sugar. Dot with butter. Bake 30 minutes.

In a small saucepan, heat the rum and pour over the bananas. Serve hot.

Can be baked for 25 minutes, allowed to cool overnight, and reheated.

Serves 8.

Minted Cantaloupe and Blueberries

½ cup sugar
1 cup water
1 tablespoon minced fresh mint

1 cup blueberries
2 cups cantaloupe balls
fresh mint sprigs

In a 1-quart saucepan, combine the sugar, water, and minced mint. Simmer 3 minutes. Strain and chill.

Just before serving, combine the syrup, blueberries, and cantaloupe in a bowl. Mix and garnish with mint sprigs.

Syrup can be prepared well ahead. Blueberries can be picked over and washed the night before. The cantaloupe should be cut into melon balls only a few hours before serving.

Serves 6.

Melon, Orange, and Blueberry Salad

3 quarts honeydew balls	2 tablespoons sugar
¾ cup orange juice	1 pint fresh blueberries
¼ cup orange-flavored liqueur	fresh mint sprigs
2 teaspoons grated orange peel	

In a large bowl, combine the melon balls, orange juice, liqueur, orange peel, and sugar. Cover and let macerate in the refrigerator for 3 to 4 hours. Add the blueberries, stir to combine, and garnish with mint sprigs.
Serves 8.
Note: You can substitute cantaloupe or any other melon, except watermelon, for the honeydew. Strawberries can be substituted for the blueberries.

Melon with Raspberry Sauce

2 quarts cantaloupe balls	¼ cup creme de cassis
¼ cup lemon juice	1 quart strawberries
2 tablespoons sugar	4 small melons, halved and seeded
10 ounces frozen raspberries, thawed	fresh mint sprigs

In a medium bowl, combine the melon balls, lemon juice, and sugar.
Puree the raspberries and their syrup in a blender or processor. Strain the mixture, discarding the seeds. Stir in the creme de cassis.
Add the strawberries to the melon balls, cover, and let macerate in the refrigerator for 3 to 4 hours. Spoon the mixture into the melon halves. Garnish with mint sprigs. Serve sauce separately.
Serves 8.

Melon de Scheherazade

1 large Persian melon	3½ tablespoons sugar
salt	¼ bottle champagne
2 slices pineapple, diced	½ cup white creme de menthe
2 peaches, sliced	¼ cup maraschino liqueur
1 banana, sliced	¼ cup kirsch
18 raspberries	butter
18 wild strawberries	

With a large knife, cut off the top third of the melon and set aside. With a melon baller, scoop out balls without breaking the shell. Scoop balls from the top piece as well. Lightly salt the melon shell and let drain, upside down on a plate, for 30 minutes. Do the same to the top piece.

In a bowl, combine the fruits, sprinkle with sugar, and macerate one hour. Drain the juices from the fruit into a bowl. Pack the fruit into the melon.

Combine the champagne, liqueurs, and fruit juice and mix well. Pour over fruits. Butter the top slice of melon and press firmly into place. Put the melon in a bowl in the refrigerator, or pack it in crushed ice for 2 hours.

Can be prepared the night before.

Serves 6.

Cherries in Sour Cream

2 pounds cherries, pitted	2 tablespoons sugar
1 ounce kirsch	1 teaspoon ground cinnamon
1 cup sour cream	grated semisweet chocolate, optional

In a bowl, combine the cherries and kirsch and mix well. Chill until ready to serve.

Beat the sour cream, sugar, and cinnamon together. Drain off 2 tablespoons of kirsch and beat into the cream. Serve the cherries topped with the sauce and grated chocolate, if desired.

Can be prepared the night before.

Serves 6 to 8.

Grapes in Brandy

3/4 cup honey	1 pound seedless grapes, washed
6 tablespoons cognac	1 cup sour cream
1 tablespoon lemon juice	

In a bowl, combine the honey, cognac, and lemon juice. Add the grapes and stir to coat completely. Chill overnight. To serve, spoon into dishes and top with sour cream.

Serves 4 to 6.

Note: You can substitute nectarines or cherries for the grapes.

Orange Chantilly

6 oranges
1 cup heavy cream
6 tablespoons sugar

2 tablespoons maraschino liqueur
6 tablespoons chopped walnuts

Cut off the top third of the oranges and scoop out the flesh, saving the juice and pulp. Free the pulp of seeds or filaments and dice. Whip the cream until stiff. Mix in the sugar, liqueur, orange pieces, orange juice, and walnuts. Mix well. Fill orange shells. Chill thoroughly.

Can be frozen in the shell. Serve garnished with orange leaves, if possible.

Serves 6.

Pesche Ripienne

6 firm, ripe freestone peaches
5 stale almond macaroons, crushed
2 egg yolks

2 tablespoons sugar
4 tablespoons unsalted butter

Preheat the oven to 375° F.

Dip the peaches into boiling water for 40 seconds and then into cold water. With a small paring knife, you should be able to peel the peaches easily. Cut the peaches in half, remove the pit, and scoop out the center pulp to make a deep shell. Chop the pulp and add it to the macaroons, egg yolks, sugar, and butter. Fill the peaches with this mixture. Arrange in a buttered baking dish, filled side up. Bake about 25 minutes, basting with pan juices. Serve warm or at room temperature.

Can be chilled and allowed to come to room temperature the next day.

Serves 6.

Note: You can use pears, nectarines, or apricots in place of the peaches.

Poires Braisees a la Bressane (Braised Pears, Bresse Style)

6 ripe firm pears, peeled
1/4 cup sugar
3 tablespoons unsalted butter
2 cups heavy cream

3 tablespoons cognac
3 tablespoons honey
1/2 teaspoon vanilla

Preheat oven to 400° F.

Cut pears in half and remove the cores. Place cut side down in a single layer in a 9 by 13 inch baking dish. Sprinkle pears with sugar and dot with butter. Bake 35 to 40 minutes, or until tender. Remove from the oven and lower heat to 350° F.

Pour 1 cup of cream over pears and return to oven for 10 minutes, or until sauce is thickened and caramel colored. Baste 3 times. Allow to cool.

Whip the remaining cream, and flavor with cognac, honey, and vanilla. Serve pears at room temperature with whipped cream on the side. Or serve hot from the baking dish without the whipped cream accompaniment.

Pears can be prepared the day before and allowed to come to room temperature.

Serves 6.

Note: You can substitute apples or peaches for the pears.

Pears and Plums in Wine

2 oranges	2-inch strip of lemon peel
¼ cup orange liqueur	3 whole cloves
8 pears	16 plums
3 cups dry red wine	3 tablespoons currant jelly
sugar	1 tablespoon lemon juice
cinnamon stick	

With a sharp knife, peel rind from the orange, without cutting into the white membrane. Cut into fine julienne and parboil for 10 minutes. Drain strips, put into a bowl, and add orange liqueur. Set aside.

Peel pears, leaving them whole with stems intact. Put into a bowl of water, acidulated with 2 tablespoons lemon juice, to cover.

In a 2-quart saucepan, combine the wine, sugar, cinnamon stick, lemon peel, and cloves. Bring to a boil and simmer until sugar has dissolved. Add pears, cover, and poach until tender, 10 to 30 minutes depending on the variety and ripeness of pears. You may have to poach the pears in batches. If so, remove the poached pears from the liquid and put into a bowl while cooking others.

When pears are cooked, add the plums to the poaching liquid. Cover and poach over low heat for 10 minutes. Remove and add to pears. Reduce remaining liquid until it is slightly syrupy. Stir in the currant jelly, lemon juice, orange peel, and liqueur. Pour over the fruit and chill.

Serves 8.

Note: You can substitute peaches or apples for the pears. Or substitute 2 quarts of strawberries for the pears and plums.

Douillons a la Paysanne (Pastry-Wrapped Baked Pears)

⅓ cup white wine	4 pears, peeled
7 ounces butter	¼ teaspoon cinnamon
salt	1 egg
2 tablespoons sugar	1 cup creme fraiche
2½ cups flour	

Preheat oven to 425° F.

In a saucepan, reduce the wine by half. Remove the pan from the heat and whisk in the butter, bit by bit, to form a creamy mixture. Add the salt, 1 tablespoon sugar, and flour to make a dough. Shape the dough into a flat cake. Wrap in waxed paper and chill in the refrigerator for 2 hours.

With an apple corer, remove the cores from the pears from the bottom. Leave the stem intact. In a small bowl, combine the remaining sugar and cinnamon and roll the pears in the mixture.

Roll the pastry ¼ inch thick and cut into 4 squares. Wrap each pear in the pastry, leaving the stem exposed. Beat the egg with a tablespoon of water and brush on each wrapped pear. Place pears in a lightly buttered baking dish. Bake 25 minutes, or until the pears are tender and the pastry is golden. Serve warm with creme fraiche.

Serves 4.

Note: You can use apples instead of pears. You also can stuff the cavities with brandied raisins, candied fruits, or ground walnuts or pecans.

Ananas Surprise (Stuffed Pineapple)

1 grapefruit	6 ounces candied cherries
2 oranges	½ cup maraschino or kirsch liqueur
2 apples	½ cup sugar
1 pineapple	

Peel the grapefruit and oranges and divide into sections. Remove the membrane. Cut sections in half. Peel the apples and dice.

Cut off the top fifth of the pineapple and set aside with leaves intact. With a long, sharp thin knife, cut straight down the inner side of the pineapple, cutting a core, leaving a ½-inch thick shell. With a small knife, cut into the pineapple about 1 inch up from the bottom. Twist the knife horizontally in one direction; remove the knife, reinsert, and twist in the opposite direction. You should be able to pull out the center of the pineapple like a large plug.

Cut the pineapple plug in half, remove the core, and cut the meat into ¾ inch dice. Put all of the fruits into a bowl and sprinkle with the maraschino or kirsch and sugar. Let macerate for 10 minutes. Pack back into the pineapple shell, cover with the top, and chill until serving time.

Can be made the night before.

Serves 4 to 6.

Note: Instead of the fruits listed, you can use 2 apricots, 4 cherries, 1 peach, 4 strawberries, and 1 tablespoon of slivered toasted almonds.

Croutes aux Prunes (Fresh Plum Toasts)

6 to 12 slices bread, ½ inch thick	12 tablespoons butter
butter	6 tablespoons brown sugar
12 to 18 plums, stoned	

Preheat oven to 350° F.

Butter the bread slices well on both sides. Place in a baking dish and arrange 5 or 6 plum halves on each slice, cut side up. Dot with remaining butter and brown sugar. Press plum halves into the bread. Cover lightly with a piece of foil and bake for 30 minutes, or until the bread is golden and crisp and the plums have a syrupy coating on top. If necessary, bake 10 minutes without the foil.

Can be prepared for baking the night before.

Serves 6.

Note: You can substitute pears, peaches, or apricots for the plums.

Flaugnarde (Baked Raisins and Prunes)

2 ounces raisins	pinch of salt
½ pound pitted prunes	½ cup flour
¼ cup cognac	1 cup milk
½ cup sugar	½ teaspoon vanilla
4 eggs	2 tablespoons butter

Preheat oven to 375° F.

Cover the raisins with cold water. Bring to a boil, remove from the heat, and let sit for 10 minutes. Drain. Cut the prunes in half. Combine the prunes and raisins in a jar and pour on the cognac. Cover tightly. Shake from time to time. In 6 to 7 hours, they should have absorbed the liquid.

In a bowl, beat together the sugar, eggs, and salt. Sift in the flour, a little at a time, stirring with a whisk. Stir in the milk, vanilla, and the entire contents of the jar. Generously butter a 9 by 13 inch gratin dish and pour in the batter. Bake for 20 minutes. Serve lukewarm from the dish.

Serves 4 to 6.

Note: You can substitute ½ pound dried apricots or pears for the prunes. Soak in cold water for 2 hours, then in cognac per the recipe.

APPENDIX
Basic Sauces and Preparations

Throughout this book, certain sauces and other preparations are used repeatedly. For easy reference, those recipes are grouped in this section. As you become more experienced in their preparation, it will not be necessary to refer to this section as often.

Bechamel Sauce

2 tablespoons butter	¼ teaspoon salt
1 tablespoon minced onion	·3 white peppercorns
4 tablespoons flour	sprig of parsley
3 cups milk, scalded	pinch of grated nutmeg

In a 1½-quart saucepan, melt the butter and saute the onion until soft, but not brown. Stir in the flour and cook the roux slowly, stirring constantly, until it looks very foamy and starts to turn golden. Stir in the milk and cook, stirring, until the mixture comes to a boil and is thickened and smooth.

Season with salt, peppercorns, parsley, and nutmeg. The sauce will be thickened at this point, but not very thick. Over low heat, simmer the sauce for 30 minutes, or until reduced to ⅔ of the original quantity. Strain.

Yields 2 cups.

Note: This sauce can be made in quantity and kept in the freezer until needed. After thawing, whisk it with a wire whip until smooth. One secret to this sauce is the long, slow cooking, which rids the floury flavor. Another secret is the straining to remove any lumps or pieces of the ingredients.

Sauce Creme (Cream Sauce)

2 cups Bechamel	salt to taste
½ cup heavy cream	lemon juice to taste

In a 1-quart saucepan, simmer 2 cups of strained Bechamel to 1½ cups. Stir in the cream and correct the seasoning with salt. If serving the sauce on fish, a few drops of lemon juice will make it more piquant. Strain.

Yields 2 cups.

Note: Can be frozen.

Sauce Aurore (Aurora Sauce)

¼ cup tomato puree, or to taste   2 cups hot cream sauce

In a 1-quart saucepan, combine the tomato puree and cream sauce and mix well.

Yields 2 cups.

Note: Can be frozen.

Sauce Mornay (Cheese Sauce)

3 egg yolks   2 tablespoons butter
½ cup heavy cream   2 tablespoons grated Gruyere or Par-
2 cups Bechamel   mesan cheese

In a small bowl, combine the egg yolks and cream. Set aside.

In a 1-quart saucepan, heat the Bechamel sauce. Transfer 4 tablespoons of hot sauce to the egg mixture and mix well. Turn the egg mixture into the remaining sauce and heat just to the boiling point. Do not boil. Stir in the butter and the cheese. Strain.

Yields about 2½ cups.

Note: Can be made the day before and reheated. Do not freeze.

Veloute Sauce

This sauce is the "other" cream sauce in fine French cooking; the principal difference is that veloute is made with stock rather than milk.

2 tablespoons butter   salt to taste
4 tablespoons flour   sprig of parsley
3 cups boiling stock   ½ cup chopped mushroom stems
3 white peppercorns

In a 1-quart saucepan, melt the butter, stir in the flour, and cook the roux until it is bubbly and just starts to turn golden. Gradually stir in the stock and cook, stirring, until it comes to a boil and is thickened slightly. Add the peppercorns, salt, parsley, and mushroom stems. Simmer, stirring often, until reduced to ⅔ of the original quantity. Strain and correct the seasonings.
Yields 2 cups.

Sauce Supreme

2 cups chicken stock	1 cup heavy cream
3 sliced mushrooms	salt and cayenne pepper to taste
1 cup veloute	

In a 1-quart saucepan, cook the chicken stock and mushrooms until reduced to ⅓ of the original quantity, or ⅔ of a cup. Add the veloute and simmer until reduced to 1 cup. Stir in the heavy cream and correct the seasoning with salt and cayenne. Strain.
Yields 2 cups.

Sauce Espagnole (Brown Sauce)

½ cup clarified butter	3 sprigs parsley
1 small carrot, minced	1 small bay leaf
2 medium onions, minced	pinch of thyme
½ cup flour	3 cups hot, unsalted beef stock
3 cups hot, unsalted beef stock	½ cup tomato puree
1 clove garlic, crushed	2 cups hot, unsalted beef stock
1 stalk celery	

In a 3-quart saucepan, melt the butter, add the carrot and onions, and cook until they start to turn brown. Stir in the flour and cook, stirring, until the roux is a rich, deep brown. Stir in 3 cups of stock, garlic, and a faggot made from celery, parsley, bay leaf, and thyme. (A faggot is virtually the same as a bouquet garni, except that the ingredients are tied between 2 4-inch-long sections of celery.)
Cook, stirring often, until the mixture thickens. Stir in 3 more cups of stock and simmer slowly for 1½ hours, or until reduced to 3 cups. As the sauce cooks, skim off any excess fat or scum on the surface. Stir in the tomato

puree and simmer 20 minutes. Strain, add the remaining hot stock, and simmer 1 hour, or until reduced to 4 cups. Cool.

Yields 1 quart.

Note: Can be frozen.

Demi-Glace Sauce

1½ cups Sauce Espagnole	5 tablespoons dry sherry
1½ cups beef stock	salt and pepper to taste

In a saucepan, combine the Sauce Espagnole and stock and simmer until reduced to 1½ cups. Remove from the heat, stir in the sherry, and strain. Correct the seasoning with salt and pepper.

Yields about 1¾ cups.

Note: Can be frozen.

Sauce Lyonnaise (Piquant Onion-Flavored, Demi-Glace Sauce)

¼ cup minced onions	½ cup wine vinegar
2 tablespoons butter	1½ cups demi-glace
2 tablespoons dry white wine	salt and pepper to taste

In a skillet, lightly brown the onions in the butter. Stir in the wine and vinegar and cook until reduced by ⅓. Stir in demi-glace and simmer 30 minutes. Season. Serve strained or unstrained.

Yields about 1½ cups.

Note: Can be frozen.

Sauce Hollandaise

3 egg yolks	salt to taste
1 tablespoon water	lemon juice to taste
½ pound butter	

In a 1-quart saucepan, combine the egg yolks and water and beat, over medium heat, with a wire whisk until light and fluffy. Beat in the butter in tablespoon portions, incorporating each before adding more. Whisk constantly, making sure that the sauce thickens before adding more. (You can melt the butter to make incorporating it easier.) Strain and correct the seasoning with salt and lemon juice.

Yields about 2 cups.

Note: This sauce can be held over warm, not hot, water for several hours. Hollandaise has a reputation of being one of the most difficult sauces to prepare. In fact, it is not difficult and if something goes wrong it can be easily corrected. If you try to add the butter too quickly, the sauce may thin out; if it gets too hot, it may curdle. In either case, put a fresh egg yolk in a warm bowl and beat the broken sauce, little by little, into the egg until incorporated and smooth.

If you wish, you can prepare the sauce in a processor or blender. Put the egg yolks and water in the processor. Melt the butter. With the machine running, pour in the butter in a steady stream until incorporated, taking no more than a minute.

Sauce Mousseline (Whipped-Cream-Lightened Hollandaise Sauce)

1 cup prepared Hollandaise	3 tablespoons heavy cream

Keep the prepared Hollandaise warm.

In a bowl, beat the cream until stiff and fold gently into the Hollandaise. Serve as soon as possible.

Yields 1½ cups.

TARRAGON-FLAVORED SAUCE MOUSSELINE   Season the Hollandaise sauce with 1 teaspoon dried, crumbled tarragon.

Bearnaise Sauce

Bearnaise is similar to Hollandaise, but it is flavored with an herbal paste.

1 teaspoon tarragon	1 tablespoon water
1 teaspoon chervil	½ pound butter
2 shallots, minced	salt to taste
¼ cup tarragon vinegar	pinch of cayenne
¼ cup white wine	1 teaspoon tarragon
3 egg yolks	1 teaspoon chervil

In a small saucepan, combine the 1 teaspoon tarragon, 1 teaspoon chervil, shallots, vinegar, and white wine. Cook over high heat until most of the liquid has evaporated and the mixture is reduced to a thick paste. Cool slightly.

Put into a medium saucepan with the egg yolks and water. Beat with a wire whisk over medium heat until the mixture is light and fluffy. Add the butter as for Hollandaise, adding no more than a third of the butter at a time. Make sure each portion is fully incorporated before adding more. Correct the seasoning with salt and cayenne pepper. Strain through a fine sieve. Add the remaining tarragon and chervil and mix well. Keep warm over hot, not boiling, water.

Yields about 2 cups.

Tomato Sauce

1 quart tomatoes, preferably plum	¼ pound butter
1 onion, halved	1 teaspoon sugar
1 teaspoon salt	salt and pepper to taste

Cut tomatoes into chunks, place in a 3-quart saucepan, and put over medium heat. Cover and simmer 10 minutes, stirring occasionally. Put tomatoes through a food mill or into a processor. If using a food processor, first force the tomatoes through a sieve to remove the seeds and skin. Discard seeds and skin.

Using a clean pot, combine the tomatoes, onion, salt, butter, and sugar. Simmer gently for 45 minutes, or until thickened and smooth. Discard the onion and correct the seasoning with salt and pepper.

Yields about 3 cups.

Note: Can be frozen.

Tomato Fondue

¼ cup minced shallots	½ teaspoon salt
1 small clove garlic, crushed	pinch of sugar
2 tablespoons butter	pinch of pepper
5 medium tomatoes, peeled, seeded, and chopped	minced parsley

In a 1-quart saucepan, cook the shallots and garlic in the butter until soft, but not brown. Add the tomatoes, salt, sugar, and pepper and cook over high heat until most of the liquid has evaporated. Stir in the parsley. The sauce should be fairly dry and pulpy.

Yields about 2 cups.

Mayonnaise

2 egg yolks	2 tablespoons vinegar, approximate
½ teaspoon salt	1 cup oil, half olive oil and half
white pepper to taste	salad oil
½ teaspoon dry mustard	

In a 1-quart mixing bowl, place the egg yolks, salt, pepper, and dry mustard along with 1 teaspoon vinegar. Whisking constantly, add the oil, drop by drop, until ¼ cup of oil has been added. Add ½ teaspoon vinegar and continue beating. Add the remaining oil in a thin stream, beating continually. If the oil should sit on the surface, stop adding it and continue beating until the oil is incorporated. Add vinegar to taste.

Will keep in the refrigerator for up to two weeks. Do not freeze.

Yields about 1¼ cups.

Note: Mayonnaise can also be made in a processor or blender. Use one whole egg rather than egg yolks. Put them into the processor with pepper, vinegar, salt, and mustard. Turn the machine on and keep it going while adding the oil in a steady stream.

Mayonnaise Collee (Jellied Mayonnaise)

1 tablespoon unflavored gelatin	2 cups mayonnaise
¼ cup cold water	

In a small saucepan, sprinkle the gelatin on the water. Let sit for 3 minutes, or until softened. Place over low heat and stir until the gelatin has dissolved. Stir into the mayonnaise.

Yields about 1 cup.

Note: This will set within a few hours in the refrigerator, so do not try to make ahead. Once used to coat the food, mayonnaise collee will protect it from becoming dry for 24 to 36 hours.

Eggplant Provencale

¾ cup olive oil
1 large eggplant, cubed
2 zucchini, diced
3 onions, thinly sliced
1 green pepper, thinly sliced
1 red pepper, thinly sliced
4 tomatoes, peeled, seeded, and
   chopped

1 teaspoon dried basil
½ teaspoon dried oregano
2 tablespoons minced parsley
2 cloves garlic, minced
salt and pepper to taste

In a 12-inch skillet, saute the eggplant in ½ cup of olive oil until browned. Drain in colander, remove, and set aside. Saute the zucchini in the remaining oil until browned. Set aside.

Add the onions, peppers, and tomatoes to the skillet and simmer until the juices have evaporated. Season with basil, oregano, parsley, garlic, salt, and pepper. Return eggplant and zucchini to the skillet and cook 5 minutes, or until tender.

Yields about 4 cups.

Note: Can be frozen and reheated.

Duxelles (Mushroom Sauce)

1 tablespoon minced shallot
3 tablespoons butter

1 pound mushrooms, minced
1 cup Bechamel

In a large skillet, saute the shallot in the butter until soft. Stir in the mushrooms and cook until the liquid has evaporated. Stir in the Bechamel and reheat.

Yields about 2 cups.

Note: Can be frozen and reheated.

Vinaigrette (Oil and Vinegar Dressing)

2 tablespoons red or white wine
   vinegar
6 tablespoons olive oil
1 teaspoon Dijon mustard

1 teaspoon lemon juice, optional
1 teaspoon salt
pepper to taste

In a bowl, combine the vinegar, oil, mustard, lemon juice, salt, and pepper. Whisk vigorously until slightly thickened.

Yields about 1½ cups.

Note: Will keep in the refrigerator for 2 to 3 weeks.

Carrot Puree

2 cups peeled, chopped carrots	¼ cup raw rice
¼ teaspoon salt	2 cups water
2 teaspoons sugar	1 tablespoon butter
1 tablespoon butter	heavy cream

In a 1-quart saucepan, combine the carrots, salt, sugar. tablespoon butter, rice, and water. Bring to a boil, cover, and simmer for 30 minutes, or until the rice and carrots are tender and the water has been absorbed. Force through a food mill or puree in a processor until smooth. Return the mixture to the saucepan and heat to dry the puree. Stir in the remaining butter and enough heavy cream to achieve the desired consistency.

Yields about 3 cups.

Note: Can be frozen.

Cauliflower Puree

1 large head cauliflower	salt and pepper to taste
¼ cup mashed potatoes, optional	1 to 2 tablespoons heavy cream
2 tablespoons butter	

Trim the cauliflower, removing the green leaves, and cut it into florets. Cook the cauliflower in boiling salted water until very tender. Drain well and force through a food mill, or puree in a processor. Stir in the mashed potatoes, if desired, and place in a saucepan. Heat until the mixture dries a little. Stir in the butter, correct seasoning with salt and pepper, and thin to desired consistency with the cream.

Yields about 3 cups.

Note: Can be frozen.

Celery Puree

2 bunches celery, chopped
2 cups chicken stock
½ cup mashed potatoes, optional

salt and pepper to taste
1 to 2 tablespoons butter

In a saucepan, cook the celery in the chicken stock for 60 minutes, or until very tender. Drain. Force the mixture through a food mill, or puree in a processor and force through a fine sieve. Heat the puree until it has dried out, or stir in mashed potatoes to help thicken it. Correct the seasoning with salt and pepper and stir in the butter.

Yields about 2 cups.

Note: Can be frozen.

Lima Bean Puree

2 10-ounce packages frozen lima
   beans
¼ cup heavy cream

salt and pepper to taste
1 to 2 tablespoons butter

In a saucepan, cook the lima beans in water to cover until very tender. Drain. Puree the beans with a food mill or in a processor. If using a processor, force through a fine sieve. Put into a saucepan and dry the mixture over heat. Stir in the cream, salt, pepper, and butter.

Yields about 2½ cups.

Note: Can be frozen.

Spinach Puree

3 pounds spinach, stripped
3 tablespoons butter

salt and pepper to taste
nutmeg to taste

Wash the spinach well, drain, and place in a saucepan with just the water on the leaves. Cover, bring to a boil, and cook and stir until just wilted. Puree in a food processor or blender until smooth. Dry over heat, and stir in the butter, salt, pepper, and nutmeg to taste.

Yields about 3 cups.

Note: Can be frozen.

Croutons

In fine cooking, croutons are slices of bread sauteed in butter or oil, not small cubes of bread dried in the oven.

6 slices white bread, ½ inch thick   2 to 3 tablespoons butter

Remove the crusts from the bread and, depending on use, cut into rounds, triangles, or other shapes. Heat the butter in a large skillet and saute the bread on both sides until golden. Drain on paper towels.

Yields 6 croutons.

Note: Best when made and served within a short period of time.

Croustades

2 loaves unsliced white bread   6 cups melted butter

Preheat oven to 350° F.

Remove the crusts from the loaves of bread and cut the bread into blocks 2½ inches wide, 4 inches long, and 2½ inches high. Cut out the center of each block, leaving ½-inch thick walls. Brush the bread on all sides with melted butter and place on a baking sheet. Bake about 20 minutes until crisp and golden brown.

Yields about 6 croustades.

Note: Best when served shortly after baking.

Pate a Chou (Cream Puff Pastry)

½ cup butter   1 cup flour
1 cup water   4 eggs
¼ teaspoon salt

Preheat oven to 400° F.

In a medium saucepan, combine the butter, water, and salt. Bring to a full rolling boil. Add the flour all at once and stir vigorously over high heat until the mixture comes together, forms a ball around the spoon, and starts to film the bottom of the pan. Remove from the heat and let cool for 4 minutes.

Put the pastry into a processor and add all of the eggs. Turn on the machine and process until smooth, stopping once or twice to stir down the egg on the sides.

To prepare by hand, beat the eggs into the cooled dough, one at a time, making sure each egg is fully incorporated before adding the next.

Fit a pastry bag with a #5 open plain tip and pipe mounds of dough onto a buttered baking sheet. For cocktail puffs, make the mounds of dough about 1 inch across. For large puffs, mounds should be about 2½ inches across. Bake until puffed and golden, about 25 minutes for small puffs and about 45 minutes for large puffs. It is advisable to pierce large puffs with a small knife after 40 minutes of baking to let the steam escape.

Yields about 75 small puffs or about 25 large puffs.

Note: Puffs freeze beautifully. Store them in plastic bags in the freezer and use as needed.

Pate Brisee Ordinaire (Pie Pastry)

3½ cups flour	20 tablespoons butter (2¼ sticks)
2 teaspoons salt	5 tablespoons (2½ ounces) lard
¼ teaspoon sugar	1 cup iced water, approximate

Put flour, salt, and sugar in a bowl. Cut the butter and lard into small pieces and toss the fats in the flour to coat well. Then use your fingertips to crumble the fats into the flour to make a coarse meal. You can use a pastry blender, if desired. Add ¾ cup water and pull the mixture together to form a mass of dough. Add more water if needed.

Turn the dough onto a board. It will look messy, but do not worry. With the heel, not the palm, of your hand, push about 2 tablespoons of the mixture away from you to about 6 inches from the outer edge of the dough. Repeat this procedure until you have pushed all of the dough across the board, smearing it. Gather the pastry together and shape it into a flat, rectangular cake about 1 inch thick. Wrap in waxed paper or put in a plastic bag and chill for at least 20 minutes.

When ready to use cut into 4 sections. On a lightly floured board, roll the dough into a square or rectangle about ¼ inch thick and 2 inches larger than the pan you are using. Lift the pastry into the pan, trim the edges, and flute decoratively, if desired. Prick the bottom of the dough lightly.

Preheat oven to 400° F.

If the shell is to be baked, line it with metal foil and fill with dried beans or rice. Bake on the middle level of the oven for about 20 minutes. Remove the beans and continue to bake to the desired degree of doneness.

This may seem like a large quantity of dough, but it is easier to handle this amount and it keeps well. Unshaped, unbaked dough will keep 3 days in the refrigerator, or up to 2 months in the freezer. You also can freeze unbaked shells, or bake them and freeze them.

Yields 4 9- or 10-inch single-crust pie shells.

Note: Think of the pastry as the warp and woof of fabric, so you only roll it in four directions rather than trying to stretch it in all directions to make a circle.

Processor Pastry Dough

2 cups flour	4 tablespoons lard
½ teaspoon salt	5 tablespoons cold water
7 tablespoons cold butter	

In the bowl of the processor, combine the flour and salt, then turn on and off once to mix. Cut the butter and lard into tablespoon-size portions and add to the bowl. With several on–off turns, process the mixture until it resembles coarse meal. With the motor running, add the water and process until the mixture is well-moistened and starting to clump together. (In the author's opinion, processing the dough until it forms a ball on top of the blades is too much.)

Remove the pastry from the bowl. Put it into a plastic bag and press gently into a flat cake. Chill 20 minutes before rolling. Roll, shape, and bake as indicated previously.

Yields enough for 1 2-crust 9-inch pie.

Sour Cream Pastry

3 cups flour	½ cup cold butter
2 teaspoons salt	¾ cup sour cream

In a bowl, combine the flour and salt. Cut the butter into tablespoon-size portions and crumble into the flour to make a coarse meal. Stir in the sour cream a little at a time, adding only enough to hold the dough together. Roll the dough into a rectangle and fold in thirds like a business letter. Chill, wrapped in waxed paper or in a plastic bag, for 30 minutes.

This dough can also be made in a processor but do not overprocess.

Yields 2 9-inch 2-crust pies.

Note: Can be frozen before or after baking.

Glossary of Terms

Many terms used in cooking have specific meanings that apply nowhere else. Moreover, various authors interpret these meanings to suit their own uses. The following are this author's interpretations of some of the terms used in this book.

BEURRE MANIE   A beurre manie is a mixture of flour and butter, used to thicken sauces, that need not be cooked first (see roux). Use equal quantities of butter and flour by *weight*. Mix them together to form a smooth paste. Shortly before the food is ready, stir pea-size pellets of the beurre manie into the simmering liquid, stirring constantly. Add only enough to thicken the sauce to the desired degree. Let the sauce come to a boil before adding more.

BOUQUET GARNI   A bouquet garni is a bag of seasoning cooked in a liquid, to give it flavor, and removed before serving. You can use a bag made of cheesecloth or old sheeting, or a stainless steel teaball. I recommend 2 sprigs of parsley, ¼ teaspoon dried thyme, 1 bay leaf, and 10 peppercorns as a generally useful bouquet garni. Change the herbs to suit your taste.

CLARIFIED BUTTER   Clarified butter results when the milk solids are removed from melted butter. The purpose is to make it possible to raise the heat of the butter without burning it. Clarified butter keeps for months in the refrigerator. Therefore, I recommend that you prepare a pound at a time. Place 1 pound of butter in a small saucepan and let it melt over low heat. When it is fully melted, remove the foam carefully from the surface and discard it. Strain the layer of oil through very fine cheesecloth wrung out in cold water. Discard the sediment at the bottom of the pan. Store in a covered jar in the refrigerator. It will be hard when cold.

TO CREAM   Butter, butter and sugar, or cream cheese are beaten to soften them and allow other ingredients to be folded into them. You can cream butter in a bowl, using a spoon or an electric mixer, or in a processor. For most of these recipes, the most efficient method is to cut the cold butter into small cubes and use a processor.

TO DEGLAZE   When food is cooked over dry heat, as in sauteing or roasting, bits of the meat and juices get stuck to the pan. They are filled with flavor. To deglaze the pan and remove those flavorful bits, add wine or stock to the pan and bring to a boil, stirring constantly. See *Glaze.*

TO DICE   Dice means to cut into even squares or cubes. Depending on the dish, the dice can be as small as ¼ inch or as large as 2 inches. Consider the end result when determining what size to make the dice.

DORURE   This is a gilding used on pastries to give them a sheen and to help them brown. You can use water, salted water, milk, cream, whole egg, egg white, egg yolk, or any mixture of these to make the dorure. The mixture with the highest fat content, heavy cream and egg yolk, gives the richest color.

TO FOLD   When ingredients have had air beaten into them, such as whipped cream or egg whites, it is important not to deflate them when adding other ingredients. Therefore, instead of stirring, fold in the ingredients. Put the lighter ingredients on top. With a wooden or rubber spatula, or even your hand, cut straight down to the bottom of the bowl, turn, and lift some of the heavier ingredients up and over the others. Turn the bowl a few inches to the left and repeat the motion, bringing more ingredients up over the top. Continue turning the bowl and folding.

TO GLAZE   Certain foods are assembled in ovenproof baking dishes and then finished under the broiler to brown and glaze them. Be careful that the food is not left under the broiler too long, since the toppings can burn very easily.

LIQUOR   Tradition refers to the juices of certain foods as liquors. For example, the juice surrounding oysters is called oyster liquor. Liquor in this sense, of course, is free of alcohol.

MINCE   Mincing is cutting food almost as finely as possible. Some writers prefer to say finely chopped. In this book, mince means finely cut dice, smaller than ¼ inch. See *Dice.*

PUREE   This refers to both a method and the result of that method. A carrot puree is made by chopping or mashing carrots until they form a smooth mass, similar to mashed potatoes. Depending on the dish and the diligence of the cook, some purees are smoother than others, for reasons of texture or finesse. The processor is excellent for making most purees. If you want an even smoother puree, force the processed puree through a fine sieve.

TO RICE   To rice is to put food through a ricer, a round metal basket with many small holes and a plunger. The ricer is used to puree potatoes and other foods, such as carrots and beets. Potatoes develop a gluey texture when mashed in a processor, but are light and fluffy when riced.

ROUX   A roux is a mixture of flour and fat, by weight, that is heated to cook the starch in the flour. Cooking the starch gets rid of the flour's taste and also helps the starch to expand and thicken the liquid when it is added.

WATER BATH (BAIN MARIE)   Many foods should be cooked gently, without browning. A water bath makes this possible. Choose a container that is at least 1 inch larger on all sides than the food container. Add enough water to reach halfway up the side of the food container. The food container can be individual custard cups, ramekins, a single large souffle dish, a charlotte mold, or similar dish.

Index